LOS CABOS

1st Edition

Where to Stay and Eat
for All Budgets

Must-See Sights
and Local Secrets

Ratings You Can Trust

Fodor's Travel Publications New York, Toronto, London, Sydney, Auckland
www.fodors.com

FODOR'S IN FOCUS LOS CABOS

Series Editor: Douglas Stallings
Editor: Douglas Stallings
Editorial Production: Evangelos Vasilakis
Editorial Contributors: Dan Millington
Maps & Illustrations: David Lindroth, *cartographer*; Bob Blake and Rebecca Baer, *map editors*
Design: Fabrizio LaRocca, *creative director*; Guido Caroti, Siobhan O'Hare, *art directors*; Ann McBride, *designer*
Photography: Melanie Marin, *senior picture editor*
Cover Photo (Cabo San Lucas): Bruce Herman/Mexico Tourism Board
Production/Manufacturing: Matthew Struble

1st Edition

ISBN 978-1-4000-1870-3
ISSN 1939-9898

SPECIAL SALES

This book is available for special discounts for bulk purchases for sales promotions or premiums. Special editions, including personalized covers, excerpts of existing books, and corporate imprints, can be created in large quantities for special needs. For more information, write to Special Markets/Premium Sales, 1745 Broadway, MD 6-2, New York, New York, NY 10019, or e-mail specialmarkets@randomhouse.com.

AN IMPORTANT TIP & AN INVITATION

Although all prices, opening times, and other details in this book are based on information supplied to us at press time, changes occur all the time in the travel world, and Fodor's cannot accept responsibility for facts that become outdated or for inadvertent errors or omissions. **So always confirm information when it matters,** especially if you're making a detour to visit a specific place. Your experiences—positive and negative—matter to us. If we have missed or misstated something, **please write to us.** We follow up on all suggestions. Contact the Los Cabos editor at editors@fodors.com or c/o Fodor's at 1745 Broadway, New York, NY 10019.

PRINTED IN THE UNITED STATES OF AMERICA

10 9 8 7 6 5 4 3 2 1

Be a Fodor's Correspondent

Your opinion matters. It matters to us. It matters to your fellow Fodor's travelers, too. And we'd like to hear it. In fact, we *need* to hear it. When you share your experiences and opinions, you become an active member of the Fodor's community. Here's how you can help improve Fodor's for all of us.

Tell us when we're right. We rely on local writers to give you an insider's perspective. But our writers and staff editors also depend on you. Your positive feedback is a vote to renew our recommendations for the next edition.

Tell us when we're wrong. We update most of our guides every year. But things change. If any of our descriptions are inaccurate or inadequate, we'll incorporate your changes in the next edition and will correct factual errors at fodors. com *immediately*.

Tell us what to include. You probably have had fantastic travel experiences that aren't yet in Fodor's. Why not share them with a community of like-minded travelers? Share your discoveries and experiences with everyone directly at fodors.com. Your input may lead us to add a new listing or a higher recommendation.

Give us your opinion instantly at our feedback center at www.fodors.com/feedback. You may also e-mail editors@ fodors.com with the subject line "Los Cabos Editor." Or send your nominations, comments, and complaints by mail to Los Cabos Editor, Fodor's, 1745 Broadway, New York, NY 10019.

Happy Traveling!

Tim Jarrell, Publisher

CONTENTS

ABOUT THIS BOOK

Our Ratings

We wouldn't recommend a place that wasn't worth your time, but sometimes a place is so experiential that superlatives don't do it justice: you just have to be there to know. These sights, properties, and experiences get our highest rating, Fodor's Choice, indicated by orange stars throughout this book. Black stars highlight sights and properties we deem Highly Recommended places that our writers, editors, and readers praise again and again.

Credit Cards

Want to pay with plastic? **AE, D, DC, MC, V** following restaurant and hotel listings indicate whether American Express, Discover, Diners Club, MasterCard, and Visa are accepted.

Restaurants

Unless we state otherwise, restaurants are open for lunch and dinner daily. We mention dress only when there's a specific requirement and reservations only when they're essential or not accepted—it's always best to book ahead.

Hotels

Unless we tell you otherwise, you can assume that the hotels have private bath, phone, TV, and air-conditioning. We always list facilities but not whether you'll be charged an extra fee to use them, so when pricing accommodations, find out what's included.

Many Listings

★	Fodor's Choice
★	Highly recommended
⊠	Physical address
⊹	Directions
⌂	Mailing address
☎	Telephone
🖷	Fax
⊕	On the Web
✉	E-mail
🖃	Admission fee
⊘	Open/closed times
Ⓜ	Metro stations
⊟	Credit cards

Hotels & Restaurants

🏨	Hotel
🛏	Number of rooms
⚴	Facilities
⦿	Meal plans
✗	Restaurant
⬘	Reservations
⤩	Smoking
🆊	BYOB
✗🏨	Hotel with restaurant that warrants a visit

Outdoors

🏌	Golf
⛺	Camping

Other

☾	Family-friendly
⇨	See also
⊠	Branch address
☞	Take note

WHEN TO GO

Although Los Cabos hotels are often busy starting in mid-October for the sport-fishing season, the high season doesn't technically begin until mid-December, running through the end of Easter week. It's during this period that you will pay the highest hotel and golf rates. Spring Break is a particularly busy and raucous time in Cabo San Lucas; if you're looking to get away from it all, this is not the time to travel here. Another busy season is the whale-watching season from January through March.

The Pacific hurricane season mirrors that in the Atlantic and Caribbean, so there is always a chance of a hurricane in Pacific Mexico from May through November. While hurricanes rarely hit Los Cabos full-on, the effects will be felt when a large hurricane hits Mexico's Pacific coast. Though rarer than Atlantic hurricanes, Pacific hurricanes do occur and can cause significant damage. Still, most summer storms are short and pass quickly, even in this so-called "rainy" season. Golfers often come to Los Cabos during the period from September through December because of the normal lack of severe storms.

Climate

In Los Cabos rain is rare, except from August to November, when the occasional hurricane brings everything to a halt. Baja Sur's winters are mild. The temperature in Los Cabos from December through April can be chilly at night (horrors!—as low as 10°C/50°F). Daytime temperatures in the winter months rise to 20°C (70°F). Summers can be hot and humid.

Forecasts **The Weather Channel** (⊕ www.weather.com).

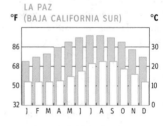

LA PAZ (BAJA CALIFORNIA SUR)

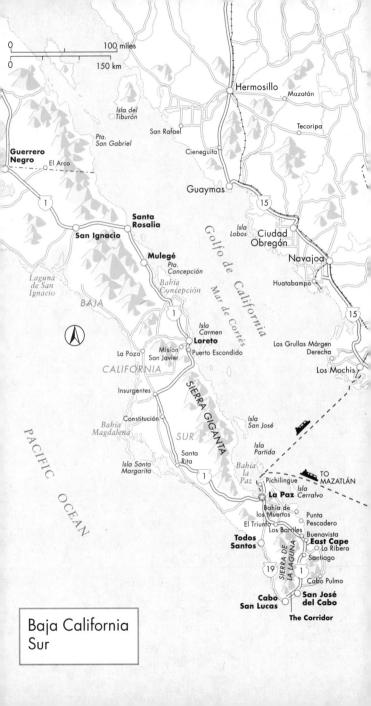

Baja California Sur

Introducing Los Cabos

WORD OF MOUTH

"Cabo is pretty safe…As for where to go, what to do, etc., Cabo is your basic beach/golf/fishing/drinking vacation spot, and there's plenty of opportunities to do all of the above. As for cost, it's relatively expensive."

—Bill_H

Updated
by Dan
Millington

WHERE DESERT AND OCEAN COLLIDE, Los Cabos sits like a sun-splashed oasis that ends at El Arco, a dramatic stone arch. To appreciate Cabo's natural beauty, look east to the sparkling aquamarine waters of the Sea of Cortez and gaze west as a fiery-orange sun descends slowly into the pounding Pacific Ocean. At the tip of Mexico's Baja peninsula, 1,669 km (1,035 mi) south of Tijuana, Los Cabos is a remote hot spot for fun seekers and sun worshippers.

Los Cabos comprises three distinct areas: the pleasant, traditionally Mexican town of San José del Cabo; outrageous, action-packed Cabo San Lucas; and, connecting the two, the Corridor—a 33-km (20-mi) strip of golf courses and resorts set amid a desert landscape. The population of Los Cabos is said to be around 50,000, although unofficial estimates inflate it to 100,000, citing the growing number of Mexicans migrating from the mainland in search of jobs and the surge of part-time residents who have purchased vacation homes.

Shops and markets overflow with manufactured ceramics, weavings, embroidered clothing, silver jewelry, and exceptional folk art from Baja and mainland Mexico. In many hotels, traditional mariachi bands entertain as you dine on Mexican fare. Without these reminders, it would be easy to forget that Los Cabos is in Mexico, as American accents far outnumber Spanish on the streets. In addition to the tourist influx, full- and part-time residents from the United States and Canada buy condos, participate in time-shares, or lease villas—whatever it takes to prolong their stay in this sunny vacationland.

Los Cabos lays claim to more than 350 days of sunshine a year. Having a day's activity spoiled by rain is rare, except from August to November, when the occasional hurricane brings everything to a halt. The climate is dry and hot, tempered by low humidity and cool breezes off the Sea of Cortez. The hottest temperatures occur from June through September, the coolest from December through April—when a sweater or jacket is usually needed in the evenings.

But there's more to enjoy than perfect weather, lovely resorts, and scenery scalloped by the Sea of Cortez. Centuries of waves crashing against the shoreline have carved out sandy coves amid huge rock outcroppings, making them perfect for swimming, snorkeling, kayaking, and scuba diving.

Baja Is Born

CLOSE UP

Los Cabos would not be a world apart today were it not for the gradual shifting of tectonic plates along the San Andreas fault, which extends north to San Francisco. The North Pacific and North American plates shifted over millions of years, creating an area where the Sea of Cortez could form. The sea slowly grew along the western side of mainland Mexico and extended north to the Colorado River. The plates gradually slid westward, forming the peninsula and the mountain ranges that create the dra-matic landscape of the Baja California Peninsula.

Baja's earliest inhabitants likely crossed the Bering Strait between Asia and North American around 50,000 BC. When Spanish explorers first encountered the region, they mistakenly believed Baja was an island. Then in 1539 an expedition sent by Hernán Cortés discovered the mouth of the Colorado River and confirmed Baja to be a peninsula. They named the waterway El Mar de Cortés (Sea of Cortez) in honor of their leader.

Fishing is still the prime water sport, whether in *pangas* (small motorized skiffs) or luxury fishing yachts. Catch-and-release is encouraged, especially for marlin, which can range from 100 pounds to more than half a ton. Between January and late March, one of the most thrilling adventures is whale-watching: gray whales migrate from the Bering Strait to winter in Cabo's warm waters, where the females give birth.

There's a lot to do on land, too. Throughout Los Cabos, new golf courses are opening almost as fast as new hotels. Some are born from the drawing boards of such famous designers as Jack Nicklaus and Tom Weiskopf. You can also hike or bike through the Sierra de la Laguna mountain range, take ATV (all-terrain vehicle) trips along the beaches and into the desert, or hit the trails on horseback.

As that golden orb kisses the western horizon, life in Cabo is only just beginning. Set off on a sunset dinner cruise, dance barefoot at a beach party, or sample dusk-to-nearly-dawn nightlife in San Lucas—the party town that some have dubbed Cabo San Loco.

THE MAKING OF LOS CABOS

Long before Spanish conquistadors arrived in the 16th century, the southern Baja peninsula was inhabited by the Guaycura people, who were divided between the Pericú and Guaycura tribes. Far less technologically developed than the indigenous peoples of mainland Mexico, the Guaycura were hunters and gatherers who lived simply in caves or crude shelters, wearing little or no clothing. The harsh environmental conditions of the southern peninsula and the constant search for food determined their lifestyle, and their isolation kept them unconcerned with building grand monuments. There are precious few signs of southern Baja's earliest inhabitants, save the chipped arrow points found in remote areas. Unlike tribes farther north, the Guaycura living around Los Cabos created little of Baja's famous rock art. Some rock paintings have been discovered in remote inland areas, but the majority of the peninsula's famous petroglyphs are in central Baja.

Spaniard Fortún Jiménez is credited with the first sighting of La Paz in what is now the state of Baja California Sur in early 1534, but Hernán Cortés is the officially recognized discoverer (May 1535). Juan Rodríguez Cabrillo explored the Pacific coastline from the tip of Baja to Santa Barbara in the mid-1500s, and his expedition team made it as far as Oregon. But the peninsula was not claimed by the Spaniards until 1663. The groundwork for the development of Los Cabos was really laid by Jesuit priests. Up to the time of their expulsion from Spain in 1768 by King Carlos III, the Jesuits had set up 17 missions north of Cabo San Lucas, including a small settlement in 1730 that was to become San José del Cabo. Nicolás Tamaral, a Jesuit priest, worked diligently to build up his mission, going into the mountains to find and convert the Pericú and other tribes; he is said to have baptized more than 1,000 Indians in his first year. Tamaral's efforts to convince the traditionally polygamous Pericú to become monogamous led to one of the largest uprisings in southern Baja. When Tamaral punished a Pericú leader for his sexual activity, the tribe revolted, killing and beheading Tamaral.

The Iglesia San José, across from the town's central plaza, was originally built in 1735, one year after Tamaral's death. The original church fell into ruins, and a new church was built on the site in the 1940s. A tile mosaic over the church entrance depicts Father Tamaral being dragged to his death. The Pericú and other indigenous groups were nearly wiped out by syphilis and smallpox, which had been introduced by waves of European settlers.

San José reached the 20th century as a successful settlement, largely due to its production of sugarcane, tomatoes, avocados, mangos, and other fruit, as well as cattle farming. At one time, more than 25,000 head of cattle roamed the countryside. From 1920 to 1930, a period known as the golden decade, large adobe homes were erected, Ford Motor cars rolled down the streets, and a dirt road was built connecting San José with Cabo San Lucas. Over the ensuing years, the town's prosperity gradually declined, due to new restrictions on shipping, bad management, and competition from other countries. San José was nearly bankrupt by the mid-1960s.

Cabo San Lucas was, for much of the 19th and early 20th centuries, just a laid-back little fishing village with few inhabitants. During World War II, pilots flying over Baja California Sur sighted large game fish in the waters around El Arco, and word of these fertile fishing grounds soon spread. In the mid-1950s, two prescient Baja aficionados constructed handsome fishing-lodge hotels with private airstrips in the Corridor. The Palmilla (rechristened the One&Only Palmilla) remains one of the most impressive resorts in Los Cabos. But the other original resort, the Hotel Cabo San Lucas, is now closed. By the mid-1960s the region had gained a reputation as one of the hottest fishing destinations in the world. A small building boom followed, attracting yacht owners and wealthy fishermen, including Hollywood celebrities Bing Crosby, Desi Arnaz, and John Wayne.

In the early 1970s, the Mexican government's tourism agency, Fonatur, acknowledged Los Cabos as a potential tourist destination. It began developing Cancún around the same time. Fonatur laid the infrastructure for Los Cabos in San José, building a hotel zone with paved streets and lighting and a nine-hole golf course. Entrepreneurs and developers saw more potential in Cabo San Lucas and the Corridor and began a building boom that has yet to end.

Preparations for the 2002 Asian Pacific Economic Conference (APEC), held in Los Cabos, included massive infrastructure improvements. A toll road was constructed between the airport and the Corridor, bridges over arroyos were built, and lines were put in for high-speed Internet access. As a result, Los Cabos has moved far into the 21st century, becoming perhaps the most modern resort area in Mexico.

PORTRAITS

THE PEOPLE

Most of the more than 75 million people living in Mexico today are descendants of native North Americans and Spaniards, with a few of African and East Asian descent whose ancestors were brought to the country as slaves. Los Cabos has its share of Spanish descendants (of the early conquistadores), but rounding out today's population are many transplants from mainland Mexico, the United States, Canada, and Europe.

Unlike other areas of Mexico with large indigenous populations—notably descendants of the Aztec, Maya, and Olmec, whose achievements can be seen in the ruins of their great stone cities—there is little evidence of the Pericú and Guaycura tribes that once inhabited Los Cabos. Some anthropologists say there are no descendants of Baja's original inhabitants in the area and that instead the ancestors of the ranchero families who populate the remote villages and towns came from northern California and the mainland or were descendants of the Spanish settlers, soldiers, and missionaries.

With its geographic separation and cultural isolation from mainland Mexico, Los Cabos differs in many respects from other Mexican resorts. The area has developed close ties to the United States (especially to California), and U.S. dollars are as common as pesos in the tourist areas. Costco and Wal-Mart have arrived, U.S. products line grocery store shelves, and U.S. investors are behind many of the large real estate developments. Many part-time and permanent residents come from California and the Pacific Northwest, as do the majority of tourists. Europeans have taken up residence here as well, investing in some of the most exciting restaurants and small hotels.

Huge numbers of workers are drawn to Los Cabos from mainland Mexico, eager to work in the construction and service industries. Unfortunately, this has caused concern about inadequate housing and facilities. Most workers live in neighborhoods tourists never see, along back streets and near Highway 19. It's clear why they come: there seems to be no unemployment in Los Cabos and the standard of living is higher than in many parts of the mainland. Begging is nearly nonexistent, and vendors selling jewelry, blankets, and hats are courteous and friendly. Mexican carpenters, bricklayers, housekeepers, waiters, lawyers, doctors, hoteliers, and other professionals seem to have unlimited prospects.

Most people who work in the tourist industry speak at least some English and are eager to learn more. In fact, the local language is basically Spanglish—a mix of English and Spanish that allows easy communication.

SPANISH GALLEONS & PIRATES

As a European settlement, Los Cabos had a raucous beginning. In 1578 Sir Francis Drake and his corsairs, backed by their English queen, were the first pirates to arrive in Los Cabos, finding its placid coves a perfect place to lay in wait for Spanish galleons. Sentinels watched for arriving ships from the highest point of the rock formation at El Arco, giving their comrades plenty of time to prepare for the attack. In the late 16th century, British, Dutch, and Chilean pirates used Chileno Bay and other coves along the Sea of Cortez as their base for preying on Spain's galleons sailing between Acapulco and the Philippines. They not only stole from the galleons but from each other, hiding the booty in caves along the coast and in the mountains. A 1,500-square-foot cave where the pirates were said to have buried some of their treasure is now included on nature walks around Hotel Cabo San Lucas.

Spain had established a regular trade route between Acapulco and the Philippines, carrying silver and gold from Mexico to Manila and bringing back silk and spices. San José del Cabo, at the time known as Aguada Segura ("place of safe water") and later as San Bernabe, was used as a shelter and provisioning point. The sailors, often sick with scurvy, could rest, pick up fresh water and food, and make any necessary repairs to their ships.

Local legend mentions a fierce English pirate called Cromwell who was said always to be favored by the winds. Ever since, whenever there is a favorable wind, it is called the *coromuel,* the local pronunciation of his name. According

The Lay of the Land

In the late 1970s, the Mexican government slated the eastern tip of Baja Peninsula Sur for upscale tourism development and gave the area from San José del Cabo to Cabo San Lucas the name Los Cabos. New hotels and opulent resorts soon sprouted up between the two towns, and residents began calling this stretch of land "the tourism corridor," which soon was shortened to "the Corridor."

About 49 km (30 mi) south of the Tropic of Cancer, Mexico's Transpeninsular Highway (Highway 1) cuts southeast to the Sea of Cortez, defining the Los Cabos area. The region's mountainous topography is dominated by three ranges: La Laguna, which tops off at 6,857 feet above sea level; San Lazaro, at 5,217 feet; and La Trinidad, at 2,920 feet. Cool winter evenings and refreshing sea breezes keep the dry desert climate temperate. Annual rainfall of 5 to 10 inches hits between August and December, with the heaviest rains in September.

to the story, Cromwell and other pirates left behind a fortune in buried treasure in the hills behind Cabo San Lucas, but none has ever been found. It's said: "Only the 'coromuel' will tell you where the treasure is buried."

George Shelvocke, who came to the Los Cabos region in 1721, recorded cultural observations and published drawings of the Pericú, describing them as "tall, straight and well formed with large arms and black, thick, poorly cared for hair." He reported both sexes as having a good appearance with a dark copper skin color. Rather than portraying the Pericú as savage, Shelvocke reported that they appeared to be endowed with all imaginable humanity and might shame some other nations. "When one of us gave something edible to one of them in particular," he wrote, "he always divided it into as many parts as there were people around, and normally reserved the smallest part for himself."

WHERE DESERT MEETS OCEAN

1

The Sea of Cortez and the Pacific Ocean, which together form a semicircle at the tip of Los Cabos, are richer in flora and fauna than the desert that forms the landmass. Still, this relatively small region has a surprising mix of terrains and flora and fauna.

Sport-fishing first put Los Cabos on the tourist map. With as many as 40,000 marlin and swordfish routinely hooked each year, the Mexican government was moved to establish strict rules governing the sport. Only one marlin, sailfish, or swordfish per fisherman a day is allowed, and anglers are strongly encouraged to return all billfish to the sea.

But the wealth of marine life goes far beyond world-record game fish. Included among the more than 850 species of fish swimming these waters are black codfish, bonito, dogfish, dorado, flounder, mackerel, rooster fish, sardines, sea bass, shark, small anchovy, tuna, and wahoo. Many varieties of mollusks and crustaceans, such as squid, clams, mussels, snail, lobster, fiddler crab, and shrimp, also live below the surface.

Fifty-foot gray whales migrate here each January, giving birth and then heading back north to the Bering Strait through early April. Colonies of seals and sea lions can be seen sunning themselves on the rocks around El Arco, one of the the only "land's ends" in the world.

Leatherback turtles, the only sea turtles without a hard shell, come ashore between November and February. More than 100 of these large reptiles (some as long as 8 feet and topping 1,200 lbs) lumber up beaches along the Corridor to scoop out a hole in the sand, where they drop their eggs during the night. Each turtle delivers about 100 eggs, which drop two or three at a time every four to 10 seconds. The mother then returns to the sea to follow her migratory path, often swimming as far away as Japan. When eggs hatch (about 56 days later), the hatchlings scramble to the sea. Many are snatched up by birds. Those that survive may return 20 or 30 years later to lay their eggs on the same beach.

In addition to the leatherback, four other species are found in Baja California: the green turtle, hawksbill, loggerhead, and olive ridley. A Los Cabos–based organization, Association Subcalifornia de Proteccional Medio Ambiente y la Tortuga Marina (ASUPMATOMA; Association for the

Protection of the Environment and the Marine Turtle in Southern Baja), raises awareness about these endangered creatures. To get involved, consult the ASUPMATOMA Web site at www.mexonline.com/tortuga.htm.

On trail hikes, you can walk through dry riverbeds at sea level up to mountains that peak near 7,000 feet to see cactus, tropical palms, and pine and oak trees growing in the same forest. Active hot springs and natural freshwater springs in the mountains disappear underground by the time they reach the foothills. Among the none-too-glamorous land fauna are coyote, wild sheep, badgers, gophers, California hare, and rice rats.

Almost half the 250 species of birds identified in Los Cabos are seacoast or open-sea birds; a small group is found in the high mountains. Species include the red-tailed hawk, black-tailed gnatcatcher, caspian tern, roadrunner, frigate bird, brown pelican, gila woodpecker, turkey vulture, osprey, quail, common ground and white-winged dove, cardinal, verdin, common yellow throat warbler, coot, and lesser nighthawk.

Nearly 3,000 plant species have been identified in Baja California, with almost 40% growing in the Los Cabos area. Of these, 275 are native to the region and found mostly on the dry and rocky hillsides. Despite an arid desert climate, Los Cabos has diverse soil types that support three general groups of vegetation: desert (mainly cacti); crops; and fruit trees. Among the 60 identified species of cacti are the plentiful cardon, said to cure toothaches and heal wounds; the pitahaya, whose fruit was a main staple of the Pericú Indians; and the giant, carrotlike cirio, native only to Baja California and Sonora. Other cactus varieties include the cholla, garambullo, palo adan, yucca, valida, and ocotillo. Common crops include strawberries, lettuces, melons, cucumbers, zucchini, and tomatoes. Mango and citrus trees, papaya, and coconut thrive near water sources, such as the San José River.

A TASTE OF LOS CABOS

For many years, it was impossible to get authentic Mexican fare in Los Cabos. Simple street stands and cafés served basic tacos, burritos, and grilled fish, along with burgers, stringy steaks, and basic pasta dishes. But the increase in tourism brought an increased demand for high-quality cuisine. Restaurants now serve authentic Mexican dishes, along with French, Spanish, Italian, Californian, Japanese, and Thai cuisine. A Baja cuisine based on fresh seafood and produce from local farms is emerging, and chefs are creating exciting combinations of Mexican and international recipes and seasonings.

Following the lead of other regions of Mexico, Los Cabos is developing individual specialties, using locally grown and raised ingredients and recipes handed down through generations. Originally, southern Baja had very few crops, but early settlers soon found pockets of fertile areas along rivers and underground springs. Many medicinal and culinary herbs are found in the mountains, and small towns such as Miraflores and Santiago cultivate some of the herbs and vegetables for Los Cabos restaurants. The road along the Pacific coast between Cabo San Lucas and Todos Santos is lined with commercial farms raising vegetables for export and for local markets and restaurants.

What Los Cabos has always had in abundance is seafood. From sea bass to tuna, mussels to squid, the fruits of the sea offer Los Cabos chefs a rich selection of ingredients for their culinary works of art. Some of the tastiest dishes are seafood soups, made with octopus, shrimp, fish, or crab. Fresh Pacific lobster is typically served simply with a butter sauce or in a salad with fresh greens. Homegrown terra fare includes local beef and pork that's marinated and often grilled or barbecued. Most of the meat served in better restaurants is imported from Sonora on the mainland or from the United States.

As the area's popularity grows, the dining-out experience is expanding to beyond just the food, with the restaurants themselves often part of the attraction. Many of San José de Cabo's eateries are in restored 19th-century adobe houses, where you can dine indoors surrounded by original art or outside amid fountains and tropical gardens in a lovely courtyard—as at **Damiana** and **Tequila Restaurante**. Adding to the international scene downtown is **Baan Thai**, whose chef, a native of Thailand, prepares authentic dishes from his homeland.

The more lively town of Cabo San Lucas has some traditional restaurants, but eating out is more often an eclectic experience. For authentic Mexican home cooking, **Mi Casa**, alongside Plaza San Lucas, is highly regarded for its regional dishes, including the *chile en nogada,* a meat-stuffed pepper topped with walnut sauce and pomegranate seeds. **Pancho's** is known for its *huevos rancheros* (fried eggs on a tortilla and topped with salsa), and **Nick San** is noted for its outstanding sushi. The **Office** on Playa Médano is the place for barefoot dining and beachside action.

Surprisingly, some of the best restaurants are in hotels. In 2004, Chicago celebrity-chef Charlie Trotter opened **C**, a chic contemporary dining room at the One&Only Palmilla resort. In downtown San José, the European-style boutique hotel Casa Natalia houses **Mi Cocina**, where French owner Loïc Tenoux and his wife Nathalie (from Luxembourg) bring their European training to traditional Mexican dishes.

PERFECT DAYS & NIGHTS

A PERFECT DAY AT THE BEACH

A perfect day on a Los Cabos beach may require only three things: wine, bread, and Gatorade—a bit of the romantic along with the practical. To keep your memories of the day perfect, add sunscreen, sunglasses, and a hat. For a small deposit, many hotels provide beach towels, coolers, and umbrellas, or you can rent these and other convenience items from **Trader Dicks** (⊠*Hwy. 1, Km 29* ☎624/142–2989), just west of La Jolla de los Cabos Resort near the Costa Azul beach. Dicks also fixes good box lunches. In winter, bring a sweatshirt or sweater to the beach.

To get to the most pristine beaches along the Sea of Cortez, head east out of San José del Cabo by car. At the corner of Boulevard Mijares and Calle Benito Juárez in San José, turn east at the sign marked PUEBLO LA PLAYA. The paved street soon becomes a dirt road that leads to the small fishing villages of **La Playa** (The Beach) and **La Playita** (The Little Beach), about 1½ km (½ mi) from San José. As of this writing, construction of a marina resort complex is underway here, but it was a long way from being completed at this writing; watch for road detours.

From La Playita, drive 60 km (37 mi) up the coast to the ecological reserve **Cabo Pulmo**, home of Baja Sur's largest coral reef. Water depths range from 15 feet to 130 feet, and it seems Mother Nature created it just for divers, snorkelers, and swimmers. Tropical fish, rays, and other colorful marine life dart along the reef and among the many shipwrecks. If you plan to scuba dive, contact **Cabo Pulmo Resort** (☎ *562/366–0398, 888/997–8566 in U.S. [answered at Cabo Pulmo]* ⊕ *www.cabopulmo.net*). When hunger pangs call, stroll up the beach from Cabo Pulmo to **Tito's** for a fish taco and an ice-cold *cerveza* (beer). Or drop by **Nancy's** in the center of town (can't miss it) for gourmet delights; it's open for breakfast, lunch, and dinner.

Try to get back to La Playa by late afternoon to avoid driving the East Cape's dirt road at night. After your hard work worshipping sun and surf, reward yourself with some fresh seafood and a frozen margarita at **Buzzard's Bar and Grill** right near the beach just north of La Playa. San José is 10 minutes away.

A PERFECT PLAY DAY

From the Cabo San Lucas marina, board one of the glass-bottom boats that depart regularly for dramatic **El Arco** (the Arch) and **Playa del Amor** (Lover's Beach), the sandy stretch in El Arco's shadow. Or head out in a kayak or tour boat from Playa Médano. The boat ride is half the fun, especially if you cruise by the sea lion colony on the rocks near the arch. The Sea of Cortez and the Pacific Ocean, which merge here, have been compared to the people of San Lucas: *cortés* (courteous) and *pacífico* (gentle). Swim and snorkel only on the Sea of Cortez side, though; the Pacific side is too rough.

There's usually a vendor or two selling water and cold drinks on the beach, but nothing more. Bring along lots of drinking water, snacks, sunscreen insect repellent, and a towel. The snorkeling is usually good around the rocks edging the sand. After a few hours on the beach, board the next boat back to the marina or paddle back to shore. This is a good time to settle in for a leisurely lunch on **Playa Médano**. The outdoor eateries along this sandy stretch are as casual and colorful as their names. Order a cold drink and a big plate of tacos or grilled fish at **Billygan's Island,** the **Office,** or **Mango Deck.**

Once you're reenergized, try parasailing, surfing, or riding a WaveRunner at Playa Médano. Activity centers on the sand rent every imaginable beach toy, along with umbrellas and lounge chairs. Head for your hotel in mid-afternoon and change into long pants for a sunset horseback ride on

Sensational Sunsets

Cabo's brilliant sunsets are best viewed from the Pacific side of Baja's tip. The Finisterra's Whale Watcher Bar and the Solmar's *palapa* (palm thatch) bar have long been favorite perches for ocean lovers any time of day. As gold and rose tint the sky, all eyes turn westward to the long, nearly empty beach and the endless expanse of natural scenery. Most sunset cruise boats glide past the land-bound onlookers. If you want to be part of the scenery, board the *Pirate* Cruise or *La Princesa*. On the Sea of Cortez side of the tip, El Arco, Cabo's famous Arch, stands out against the sunset's glow. Claim one of the cliff-top tables at Ristorante Sunset Da Mona Lisa Italian Restaurant for spectacular panoramas, or join the revelers praising the fading light at one of Playa Médano's beach bars. One of the best ways to enjoy the sunset in San José del Cabo is to go horseback riding on the beach. This can be arranged at most of the hotels.

the beach. Both **Red Rose Riding Stables** and **Cuadra San Francisco** have horses for all levels of riders. After the sun sets, dine at one of San Lucas's rock-and-roll hangouts.

A PERFECT DAY OF SIGHTSEEING

For first-timers trying to get a feel for the area, it's a good idea to take an organized sightseeing tour at the beginning of the vacation. If you're ready to set out on your own, start your tour at **La Fábrica de Vidrio Soplado** (Blown-Glass Factory)—a bit hard to find if you're driving yourself. First head toward San José on Avenida Cárdenas, which turns into Highway 1. Turn left at the stoplight and signs for the bypass to Todos Santos; then look for signs to the factory. The factory is in an industrial area two blocks northwest of Highway 1. Most taxi drivers know the way and charge about $8 from Cabo San Lucas. At the factory, you can watch artisans, who produce more than 450 pieces a day, use a process that has changed little since it was first developed some 4,000 years ago. The on-site store sells many of these pieces. Admission is free, but you can drop a donation in the bowl near the artisans.

From the factory, head east on Highway 1 for the 20-minute drive to San José del Cabo. In San José, stop for an authentic, inexpensive Mexican lunch at **La Cenaduría** (Av.

Zaragoza and Plaza Mijares). Park at the south end of Boulevard Mijares around the Tropicana restaurant, since traffic tends to get congested in the next few blocks. Take your time wandering through the shops on Mijares, and then settle in at a table in the restaurant's courtyard. Try the mixed-seafood specialty Las Cazuelas, which is cooked in a clay pot.

After lunch, stroll across the street to the plaza in front of the **Iglesia San José** (mission church) and join the locals in this tree-shaded square. Everything in San José moves at a slow pace, so don't feel guilty if all you feel like doing is wandering in and out of shops and art galleries.

Return to your hotel for dinner or try **Mi Cocina** (☎ 624/142–5100; reservations essential), an outdoor restaurant at the Casa Natalia hotel (at the north end of Boulevard Mijares). European dishes with a Mexican flair are served amid dramatic lighting, cascading waterfalls, and flaming braziers.

A PERFECT DAY IN TODOS SANTOS

For a respite from the bustling crowds of Los Cabos, head 45 minutes north of San Lucas along Highway 19 to this small, laid-back town. The Águila bus that leaves the San Lucas terminal every two hours is more comfortable and less expensive than trips offered by tour operators—though a cab to the bus station can cost $8 from downtown San Lucas. No announcements are made, so get off when the bus stops at **Pilar's Fresh Fish Tacos,** or you'll wind up in La Paz. Cross the street and walk up Avenida Zaragoza to Benito Juárez.

Continue along Benito Juárez to the gorgeously restored **Hotel California.** Turn left at the corner of Calle Máquez de León to see the **Misión de Nuestra Senora del Pilar** (Mission of Our Lady of Pilar). Off to the right, on Calle Centenario, is the **Café Santa Fé,** one of the first buildings in Todos Santos to be renovated, starting a trend that revived the area. The café has a beautiful garden and serves organic dishes. Along any street, explore interesting cafés, shops, and galleries. Stop by **El Tecolote Bookstore,** on the corner of Benito Juárez and Calle Hidalgo, for a free copy of *El Calendario de Todos Santos,* with articles on local artists and reviews of restaurants, shops, and galleries.

To take the bus back to Los Cabos, walk east toward the ocean on Benito Juárez to Avenida Zaragoza, and turn left. Walk one block and wait on the corner in front of the park. You can pay ($9) on board in pesos or dollars. Take a taxi back to your hotel from the San Lucas station.

Exploring
Los Cabos

WORD OF MOUTH

"What an amazing sight. El Arco takes your breath away. It's so beautiful, and worth every penny to see it up close in a boat! Plus the seals are so cute."

—Christina

Updated
by Dan
Millington

IF BASKING IN THE SUN, hauling in a record billfish, or roaring over sand dunes on an ATV become old hat, consider a leisurely day of sightseeing instead. Although Los Cabos is known more for beach- and bar-side action than for sightseeing, it nevertheless does hold its share of cultural and historic points of interest.

A day spent in either Cabo San Lucas or San José del Cabo can be a stroll that simply follows your whims, or an organized tour led by a local guide. A few tour operators run day trips through the two towns, as well as more adventurous treks through outlying areas, including the East Cape. If you would rather skip terra firma and ride the waves, boat tours from the marina in San Lucas include a pirate-ship adventure, whale-watching, and sunset cruises. Cruises can be booked through your hotel, or you can go to the Cabo San Lucas Marina before 4 PM to see what's available.

Note that some sightseeing tours lack knowledgeable guides. It's especially a problem when drivers double as guides—you're often encouraged to wander around on your own instead of being led to an interesting museum, historical site, or unusual shop. To ensure a worthwhile tour, request an itinerary beforehand and make sure everything you want to see is listed.

Numbers in the margin correspond to points of interest on the Cabos San Lucas and San José del Cabo maps.

SAN JOSÉ DEL CABO

The municipal headquarters for Los Cabos, San José has a population of about 25,000. The hotel zone is on a long stretch of waterfront facing the Sea of Cortez; an 18-hole golf course and a private residential community have been established south of town center. The downtown area, with its adobe houses and jacaranda trees, still maintains the languid pace of a Mexican village, though bumper-to-bumper traffic sometimes clogs the streets during weekday business hours. Despite recent hotel development, San José remains the more peaceful of the Los Cabos towns—the one to come to for a quiet escape.

Hotels along the Paseo Malecón San José (the coastal strip between where Highway 1 curves north and the Paseo Malecón ends, at the Hotel Presidente InterContinental)

San José del Cabo

↑ TO
LA PAZ AND AIRPORT

Ignacio Comonfort

Av. Zaragoza

Av. Manuel Doblado

M. Castro

Coronado

Margarita Maza de Juárez

Cerro de la Cruz

Valerio Gonzalez Canseco

Carretera Transpeninsular

Moretos

Miguel Hidalgo

Blvd. Mijares

Boulevard
Mijares, 1

Casa de la
Cultura, 5

Iglesia
San José, 3

El Palacio
Municipal, 4

Plaza
Mijares, 2

Cerro de
El Vigía

Club de Golf

0   250 meters

0   250 yards

TO
CABO SAN LUCAS

Playa Hotelera

Mar de Cortés

are about a 15-minute walk from most restaurants and shops. A taxi from the hotels to downtown costs about $6 each way. There's a taxi stand on Boulevard Mijares near Plaza Mijares. If you're staying in San Lucas or the Corridor and want to explore the San José area, you may want to rent a car. Parking is usually available around the town center.

TIMING

Unless you want to devote a lot of time to shopping, the town of San José can easily be seen in a half day and can be paired with a side trip to **Santiago** (⇨ *Off the Beaten Path, below*). To avoid driving after dark, it's best to go to Santiago first, returning to explore San José on foot in the late afternoon and/or early evening.

WHAT TO SEE

❶ **Boulevard Mijares.** The main street in San José del Cabo, Mijares is lined with restaurants and shops; the fountain in the center median is illuminated at night. The south end of the boulevard has been designated the tourist zone, with the Los Cabos Club de Golf as its centerpiece. The boulevard

A GOOD TOUR

Driving in from San Lucas or the Corridor, follow Paseo Malecón San José to **Boulevard Mijares** and park near **Plaza Mijares**. A good choice for lunch is the Damiana Restaurant, housed in an 18th-century house off the northeast corner of the plaza. You can eat outside under a tree, inside surrounded by antiques, or on the back patio amid flowering bougainvillea. Linger over lunch, as some shops close from noon to 2 PM.

After a relaxing lunch, set out to explore San José on foot. It's impossible to get lost in this easy walking town: simply look up for the church's twin spires, visible from any point, and you'll have found the main plaza. The length of your walk will depend on how much time you spend in the shops. Stop in first at the **Iglesia San José** on Zaragoza at Morelos. Walk east along Zaragoza, visiting the shops surrounding the plaza, and head south down Boulevard Mijares. At the corner of Avenida Manuel Doblado is **El Palacio Municipal,** which you can recognize by its clock tower. Continue as far as you like along Boulevard Mijares; then cross to the other side and work your way back to the plaza. At the far end of the boulevard, past many intriguing shops, is the **Casa de la Cultura.** If you're thirsty from your walk, stop next door for a drink in the lovely courtyard of the Casa Natalia hotel. Several excellent restaurants and a few galleries line the streets just north of the plaza. This neighborhood is worth exploring for new discoveries.

ends at Paseo Malecón San José, where a few reasonably priced hotels and large all-inclusive resorts face a beautiful, long stretch of beach that's perfect for morning strolls (the surf, unfortunately, is too rough for swimming).

❺ Casa de la Cultura *(House of Culture).* During the 1847 War of Intervention, this simple terra-cotta–color building served as a refuge for a company of American sailors. It now occasionally hosts theater, music, and dance performances. ⊠*Blvd. Mijares and Obregón* ☎*No phone* ⊙*Mon.–Sat. 9–8.*

NEED A BREAK? The sidewalk café at the **Tropicana Bar and Grill** (⊠*Blvd. Mijares 30* ☎*624/142–1580*), near Plaza Mijares, is a favorite tourist hangout. Walk around to the back to see the gardens and the lovely indoor restaurant. It was once a 19th-century home, as were many of the buildings in San José del Cabo.

❸ Iglesia San José. The town's twin-spired 1940 church looms above Plaza Mijares. This was originally the site of a Jesuit mission erected in 1735, one year after Pericú Indians decapitated the Jesuit priest Father Nicolás Tamaral. A tile mural over the church entrance shows him being dragged toward a raging fire. ⊠*Zaragoza at Morelos* ☎*No phone* ⊙*Daily dawn–dusk.*

❹ El Palacio Municipal *(City Hall).* Built in 1891, this modest yellow-and-white building near Plaza Mijares has a conspicuous clock tower. ⊠*Blvd. Mijares and Zaragoza* ☎*No phone* ⊙ *Weekdays 9–5.*

❷ Plaza Mijares. Locals and travelers mingle at the large central plaza, where a white wrought-iron gazebo and forest-green benches are set in the shade. The plaza has a small stage and plenty of space for art shows and celebrations. ⊠*Bounded by Blvd. Mijares, Hidalgo, Obregón, and Zaragoza.*

OFF THE BEATEN PATH **Santiago.** This small ranching and farming town (population 2,500), settled by the Jesuits in 1724, is 52 km (32 mi) north of San José del Cabo—about a one-hour drive. Turn off Highway 1 at Km 84, just north of the large cement ball that marks the line of the Tropic of Cancer. You should soon see orchards as well as vegetable and sugarcane fields, before arriving at Santiago's town square surrounded by old adobe homes.

Calle Guadalupe Victoria, the main street that takes you to the town plaza, will bring you past several sights. The **Parque Zoológico Santiago** (*Santiago Zoo* ⊠*Calle Guadalupe Victoria s/n* ☎*No phone*), open daily 6–6, serves as a sanctuary for animals and birds that have been injured and can no longer survive in the wild. A few native species, including white-tailed deer, coyote, and an eagle, can also be seen here. The modest zoo doesn't charge admission, but donations are appreciated. On the corner of Calzada Maestros Misioneros de 1930 and Calle Victoria is the town's twin-spired Catholic church, erected in 1735 and since rebuilt. Next to the church is Santiago's small museum (no phone), open daily 8–1; it houses artifacts, but the main attractions are fossils of giant clams, reptiles, fish, and turtles—all inhabitants of the area millions of years ago when the entire peninsula was underwater.

For a leisurely lunch, the restaurant in the garden of the small, rustic **Palomar Hotel** (✉ *Calzada Maestros Misioneros de 1930* ☎ *No phone*) is the perfect spot. Credit cards are not accepted. Just outside Santiago are three **hot springs**—El Chorro, Santa Rita, and Agua Caliente—where you can relax and rejuvenate in a pool large enough to seat 25 people. To get to the hot springs, stay west on Calle Victoria (it turns into a dirt road) for about 7 km (4 mi). About 45 minutes northwest of Santiago along Calle Victoria (at this point a dirt road) is an **Indian rock-art site,** a massive exposed boulder bearing rare, dramatic "handprint" artwork.

CABO SAN LUCAS

Once an unsightly fishing town with dusty streets and smelly canneries, Cabo San Lucas has become Los Cabos's center of tourism activity. The sport-fishing fleet has its headquarters here, and cruise ships anchored off the marina discharge passengers into town. Trendy restaurants and bars line the streets, and massive hotels have risen on every available plot of waterfront turf. Always bustling, San Lucas elevates people-watching to a world-class sport— one that can keep you entertained for hours.

After you've wandered in and out of shops, visited the glass factory, played in the surf, and developed a ruddy glow from too much sun, it's time for some serious sightseeing. Though most of San Lucas can be seen by foot, it's worth taking a water taxi or glass-bottom boat out to El Arco (The Arch) and Playa del Amor (Lover's Beach) for a closer look.

Many restaurants and bars in this party town are more than a place to eat and drink, they are sights to see—often hysterical, not historical, and with names as whimsical as their facades. A few of these are Cabo Wabo, El Squid Roe, and the Giggling Marlin. *See the Nightlife and the Arts chapter for descriptions of these multifaceted attractions.*

Allow a full day to take in Cabo San Lucas at a comfortable pace. It's best to walk along the uphill and downhill

Cabo San Lucas

streets between Boulevard Marina and Plaza San Lucas in the early morning or late afternoon, when it isn't so hot. When the cruise ships drop anchor, San Lucas's streets get crowded, especially during high season.

WHAT TO SEE

Cabo San Lucas Harbor. The boot-shape harbor is the focal point for San Lucas's boating community. Many sport-fishing boats pick up anglers at the docks at the south end of the marina, where water taxis and glass-bottom boats also dock. Some sport-fishing companies use the marina behind the Tesoro Resort Hotel, which is also used by most of the large tour boats, while others depart from the marina near the now closed Hotel Hacienda. A third marina at the north end of the harbor is filled with gorgeous private yachts. Vendors wander along the harbor walkway hawking fishing trips, sunset cruises, and, of course, time-shares.

🕧 **El Arco.** The most spectacular sight in Cabo San Lucas, this natural rock arch is visible from the marina and from some hotels, but it's most impressive from the water. If you don't take at least a short boat ride out to the Arch and Playa del

A GOOD TOUR

Start your walking tour from in front of cream-color Tesoro Resort on Boulevard Marina, in front of the Cabo San Lucas Marina. Head up Calle Hidalgo to Avenida Cárdenas and Plaza Amelia Wilkes, more commonly called **Plaza San Lucas.** This is a pleasant spot to absorb the passing scene of locals and tourists browsing in the galleries, bars, and restaurants. Stop in at the modest **Museo de las Californias** with a giant whale skeleton out front. Displays on fossils and Cabo's history are interesting, and museum volunteers are continuing to add to the collection. Just beyond the plaza, on Calle Cabo San Lucas between Calles Madero and Zapata, stands **La Parroquia de San Lucas,** the town's parish church.

Walk back down Hidalgo toward the Bahía de Cabo San Lucas (Cabo San Lucas Bay) and then turn right on Boulevard Marina. A walkway runs along the water's edge and the **Cabo San Lucas Harbor,** where boats dock at several marinas. The traditional docks for fishing boats line the south side of the marina near the end of Boulevard Marina. Sport-fishing boats usually start returning around 1 PM, and anglers tend to hang around bragging about their hauls. It's a rare day that a fishing boat returns empty-handed. The color of the flags flying from the boats tells you if they have caught a marlin: if it's blue, one's aboard; if red, it was caught and released. Browse through the crafts stalls near the docks at the **Mercado de Artesanías.** Vendors at the market are willing to barter over their prices, especially when there aren't any cruise ships in port.

For a cool drink and more shopping, walk north around the bay, past the Tesoro Resort to the shops and restaurants at **Plaza Bonita and Puerto Paraíso.** You can snack on everything from tapas to Häagen-Dazs while surveying the lineup of million-dollar private yachts and fishing boats in the marina. After refueling, continue around the bay to **Playa Médano.** Linger to watch the beach action or simply take in the view of **El Arco** from one of the open-air cafés.

If you have any energy left, continue your tour with a boat ride out to El Arco. Water taxis and glass-bottom boats pick up passengers at Playa Médano (or at the Cabo San Lucas Marina). An exhilarating way to end your day is with a sunset ride on horseback or ATV to **El Faro de Cabo Falso,** the remains of a 19th-century lighthouse.

The End Is Near

Dramatic photos of **El Arco** (the Arch), that starkly beautiful geological rock formation at the tip of Baja California Sur, have turned it into as recognizable a symbol of Mexico as the great Maya ruins of the Yucatán. The arch marks the place where the placid waters of the Sea of Cortez clash with the pounding Pacific Ocean.

Adding to the Arch's postcard appeal is **Playa del Amor** (Lover's Beach), the somewhat secluded stretch of sand that fans out around El Arco. Rumor has it that the amorous label originated as a joke: the beach was only big enough for two people. Increasing popularity could soon make the label a misnomer.

Amor, the beach underneath the Arch, you haven't fully appreciated Cabo.

❸ El Faro de Cabo Falso (*Lighthouse of the False Cape*). The abandoned shell of a lighthouse built in 1890 sits amid sand dunes, some more than 500 feet high, and overlooks the cape and a 1912 shipwreck. To reach the lighthouse by land, you need an ATV, a four-wheel-drive vehicle, or a horse. A dirt road slightly north of San Lucas, off Highway 19, leads to the lighthouse and a secluded beach where turtles come ashore to lay their eggs.

❽ La Parroquia de San Lucas (*St. Luke's Catholic Church*). The original church on this site was founded by the Jesuits in about 1740. The current church is a simple and solemn structure that's constantly being remodeled and enlarged. ⊠*Av. Cabo San Lucas, between Madero and Zapata* 🕾*No phone* ⊙*Daily dawn–dusk.*

❾ Mercado de Artesanías (*Crafts Market*). Mexican crafts, from pottery and blankets to shawls and sombreros, are sold here. Treasures include wood carvings of marlin and whales. You can arrange a glass-bottom boat ride here. ⊠*Cabo San Lucas Marina, south end of Blvd. Marina* ⊙*Daily 8* AM*–9* PM.

❼ Museo de Las Californias. The white skeleton of an adult gray whale stretches in front of this small but growing museum dedicated to the archaeology and culture of the Baja Peninsula. Exhibits include a collection of fossils, pottery, and ranching implements. ⊠*Av. Hidalgo, across from Plaza San Lucas* 🕾*624/143–0187* 🔁*$1* ⊙*Tues.–Sat. 8–3.*

⑭ Playa Médano. The most popular stretch in Los Cabos for sunbathing and people-watching, this 3-km (2-mi) span of tan sand is typically crowded, especially on weekends. More active types can rent Jet Skis and sea kayaks, go parasailing, or work up a sweat jogging. After all this exercise—even if it's just your eyes that are tired from watching everyone else—relax at one of the beachfront eateries: **Mango Deck** (☎624/143–0901), **Billygan's Island** (☎624/143–4830), or the **Office** (☎624/143–3464).

Getting to Médano in the early morning—the only time this beach even hints at serenity—could reward you with crowds of migrating whales far offshore, especially January through April.

⑩ Plaza Bonita. On the waterfront at the beginning of Boulevard Marina, this pretty bi-level plaza has some of the nicest shops in town. Several restaurants line its waterfront area. ⊠*Bordered by Blvd. Marina and Av. Cárdenas.*

⑥ Plaza San Lucas. The main downtown street, Avenida Lázaro Cárdenas, passes this pretty plaza (also called Plaza Amelia Wilkes) with a white wrought-iron gazebo. The center of the tourist part of town, it's surrounded by shops and restaurants.

⑪ Puerto Paraíso. The view of the marina has forever been changed by this enormous, elegant complex, which will eventually include a shopping mall, hotels, condos, a spa, and a convention center. At this writing, the shopping mall is open and filling with franchise restaurants (Johnny Rockets, Ruth's Chris Steak House, Häagen-Dazs) and boutiques hawking sportswear, jewelry, and souvenirs. ⊠*Av. Cárdenas at Blvd. Marina* ☎624/143–0000.

Where to Eat

3

WORD OF MOUTH

"My favorite place in Cabo San Lucas is Mi Casa—no view, but I love the *carnitas Michoacan*. I also have enjoyed Edith's, which is very expensive. There is no view, but it is set up in a neat palapa."

—MichelleY

Updated
by Dan
Millington

AFTER A LONG NIGHT of barhopping and dancing, the couple had one thing on their minds—tacos. Turning off the main street, they slid into a 24-hour taquería and scanned a bible of choices. Tired and a little bleary-eyed, it took them a few minutes: beef, chicken, shrimp, sea bass? Cactus flower, squash blossom, haban-what? A little salsa, a drizzle of chili sauce, and their sizzlin' night just got hotter.

From elegant dining rooms to casual seafood cafés to simple taquerias, Los Cabos serves up French, Italian, Japanese, Thai, vegetarian, kosher, and, of course, Mexican cuisine. Unfortunately, most restaurants try to please everyone and overcome fierce competition by offering similar menus with often mediocre results. But a few chefs and restaurateurs have found their niches and their audiences. The food scene changes quickly, and a place that shines one month may be only satisfactory the next. It's always a good idea to ask fellow travelers about their dining experiences.

Seafood is the truly local cuisine. Fresh catches that land on area menus include dorado (mahimahi), *lenguado* (halibut), *cabrilla* (sea bass), *jurel* (yellowtail), and marlin. Native lobster, shrimp, and octopus are particularly good. Fish grilled over a wood fire is perhaps the most indigenous dish. The most popular may be the *taco de pescado* (fish taco), which has many variations but is traditionally a deep-fried fillet wrapped in a handmade corn tortilla, served with shredded cabbage, cilantro, and sauces. Beef and pork, commonly served grilled and marinated, are also quite good. Many restaurants import their steak, lamb, duck, and quail from Sonora, Mexico's prime pastureland.

In San José, several international chefs prepare excellent Continental, Asian, and Mexican dishes in lovely restaurants. The Corridor is the place to go for exceptional hotel restaurants. San Lucas has comfort food covered, with franchise eateries from Domino's to Carlos 'n' Charlie's to Ruth's Chris Steakhouse.

ABOUT THE RESTAURANTS

Restaurants generally don't stay open late; if you arrive after 10 PM, you're taking your chances. Most are open year-round and only close one night a week, typically Sunday or Monday. Unless otherwise noted, the restaurants listed in this guide are open daily for lunch and dinner. In this chapter, reservations are mentioned only when they're essential, but it's a good idea to make reservations everywhere during high season. You may have to wait a half hour or so at the popular restaurants that don't take reservations. Dress is casual. Polo shirts and nice slacks are fine even in the most upscale places; shirts and shoes (or sandals) are a must except on the beach.

Restaurants in Los Cabos tend to be pricey, even by U.S. standards. Some places add a 15% service charge to the bill and some add a fee for credit-card usage. If you wander off the beaten path—often only a few blocks from the touristy areas—you can find inexpensive, authentic Mexican fare (though still more expensive than elsewhere in Mexico). The restaurants we list are the cream of the crop in each price category.

WHAT IT COSTS IN U.S. DOLLARS				
AT DINNER				
$$$$	$$$	$$	$	¢
over $30	$20–$30	$12–$20	$8–$12	under $8

Prices are per person for a main course at dinner, excluding service charges or taxes.

SAN JOSÉ DEL CABO

San José's downtown is lovely, with adobe houses and jacaranda trees. Entrepreneurs have converted many of the old homes into stylish restaurants.

AMERICAN

$-$$$ ✕**Tropicana Bar & Grill.** Start the day with coffee and French toast at this enduringly popular restaurant. The back patio quickly fills for every meal with a loyal clientele that enjoys the garden setting. The menu includes U.S. cuts of beef and imported seafood along with fajitas, chiles rellenos, and lobster—always in demand. San José's nightlife scene revolves around the second-story bar. Latin bands and other musicians play nightly. ⊠*Blvd. Mijares 30, Centro* ☎*624/142–1580* ☐*AE, MC, V.*

¢-$$ ✕**Buzzard's Bar & Grill.** Fronted by miles of secluded beach,
★ this casual seaside cantina gets rave reviews from locals who drive out to escape the Los Cabos madness. Former Southern California restaurant owners Denny and Judie Jones serve up hefty steaks, seafood dinners, and burgers,

San José del Cabo Dining

El Ahorcado
Taqueria, **9**

Baan Thai, **7**

Buzzard's
Bar & Grill, **1**

El Chilar, **2**

Damiana, **5**

French Riviera
Patisserie, **8**

Mi Cocina, **6**

La Panga
Antigua, **10**

Tequila
Restaurante, **3**

Tropicana
Bar & Grill, **4**

plus a Sunday breakfast that's a big hit. To get here, turn off
Boulevard Mijares at the signs for La Playa and follow the
road up the hill past La Playa; it's about 10 minutes from
San José in the Laguna Hills neighborhood. ⊠*Old East
Cape Rd.* ☎*702/255–0630 in U.S.* ▭*No credit cards.*

CAFÉS

¢–$ ✕**French Riviera Patisserie.** Just try to resist the croissants
and éclairs in glass cases beside displays of candies and
ice creams. Wander back to the creperie area, where the
cook tucks fresh crepes around eggs and cheese, ground
beef and onions, or shrimp and pesto sauce. Chicken salads, quesadillas, and other sensible dishes are served at
tall and short tables. There are fine wines and tequilas.
⊠*Manuel Doblado at Hidalgo, Centro* ☎*624/142–3350*
▭*AE, MC, V.*

CONTINENTAL

$–$$$ ✕**Damiana.** At this small hacienda beside the plaza, past
the center of town, bougainvillea wraps around tall pines
that surround wrought-iron tables, and pink adobe walls
glow in the candlelight. Start with fiery mushrooms *dia-
blo* (mushrooms steeped in a fiery-hot sauce), then move

on to the tender chateaubriand, charbroiled lobster, or the signature shrimp steak made with ground shrimp. ⊠*Blvd. Mijares 8, Centro* ☎*624/142–0499* ⊟*AE, MC, V.*

ECLECTIC

★ Fodor'sChoice ✕**Mi Cocina.** Visiting chefs and foodies favor
$$–$$$ this chic outdoor restaurant at Casa Natalia, Cabo's loveliest boutique hotel. Torches glow on the dining terrace, and the tables are spaced far enough apart so that you don't have to share your sweet nothings with a neighbor. Chef-owner Loic Tenoux plays with his ingredients, mixing marinated octopus with Chinese noodles in a to-die-for salad and stuffing poblano chiles with lamb and Oaxacan cheese. His fried Camembert goes well with many of the imported wines on the extensive list. ⊠*Casa Natalia, Blvd. Mijares 4, Centro* ☎*624/142–5100* ⊟*AE, MC, V.*

$–$$$ ✕**Tequila Restaurante.** An old adobe home sets the stage for
★ a classy dining experience. A lengthy tequila list gives you a chance to savor the finer brands of Mexico's national drink, and the menu challenges you to decide between excellent regional dishes and innovative Pacific Rim spring rolls, salads, and seafood with mango, ginger, and citrus sauces. Take your time and sample all you can. ⊠*Manuel Doblado s/n* ☎*624/142–1155* ⊟*AE.*

MEXICAN

$$$–$$$$ ✕**La Panga Antigua.** A wooden *panga* (small skiff) hangs
★ above the door at this intriguing restaurant. Tables are on a series of patios, one with a faded mural, another with a burbling fountain. Chef Jacobo Turquie prepares a superb catch of the day, drizzled with basil-infused oil and served with sautéed spinach and mashed potatoes. His regional seafood and chilled mango soups are also exceptional. ⊠*Calle Zaragoza 20, Centro* ☎*624/142–4014* ⊟*AE, MC, V.*

★ Fodor'sChoice ✕**El Chilar.** The fine selection of Mexican wines
$$–$$$ and tequilas suits the stylish menu at this small restaurant, where murals of the Virgin of Guadalupe adorn bright orange walls. In his open kitchen, chef Armando Montaño uses chilies from all over Mexico to enhance traditional and continental dishes (without heating up the spice), coating rack of lamb with ancho chile and perking up lobster bisque with smoky *chiles guajillos*. ⊠*Calle Juárez at Morelos* ☎*624/142–2544* ⊟*No credit cards* ⊙*Closed Sun. No lunch.*

¢–$ ✕**El Ahorcado Taquería.** By day it looks like a hole in the
★ wall, but by night this open-air eatery comes to life. It's
one of the few area restaurants open late, and it stays
packed until closing, usually around 3 AM. Old pots, baskets, antique irons, sombreros, and the like hang from the
walls and rafters. Tacos and enchiladas come with such
tasty fillers as *flor de calabaza* (squash blossom), *nopales*
(cactus flower), and *rajas* (poblano chilies). It's a bit outside the town center, so you need to drive or take a taxi.
✉*Paseo Pescadores and Marinos* ☎624/148–2437 ═No
credit cards ☉Closed Mon.

THAI

$–$$ ✕**Baan Thai.** The aromas alone are enough to bring you
★ through the door, where you're then greeted with visual
and culinary delights. The formal dining room has Asian
antiques, and a fountain murmurs on a patio. The chef
blends Asian spices with aplomb, creating sublime pad
thai, lamb curry, and the catch of the day with lemon
black-bean sauce. Prices are reasonable for such memora-
ble food. ✉*Morelos and Obregón, across from El Encanto
Inn, Centro* ☎624/142–3344 ═MC, V.

THE CORRIDOR

With a few exceptions, dining in the Corridor is restricted
to hotel restaurants.

AMERICAN

$$$–$$$$ ✕**C.** Famed Chicago chef Charlie Trotter is behind this
restaurant in the One&Only Palmilla resort. Cylindri-
cal aquariums separate the open kitchen from the dining
room. An open-air bar has seating areas overlooking the
rocky coast. Trotter's menu emphasizes vegetables—salsify,
wax beans, turnips—and pairs short ribs with parsnips and
beets or rabbit with a sweet chili sauce. There's an awe-
some chocolate soufflé for dessert. The menu changes daily.
✉*One&Only Palmilla, Carretera 1, Km 27.5* ☎624/146–
7000 ♨*Reservations essential* ═AE, MC, V ☉No lunch.

¢–$$ ✕**Central Gourmet.** At this deli-restaurant breakfast might
be a spinach, egg, and bacon burrito, and lunch and dinner
might consist of a gourmet pizza, Cajun chicken salad, or
sushi. Pick up a picnic meal before heading to the beach
or sit back on the deck and watch the steady stream of
locals stopping by for takeout meals. ✉*Carretera 1, Km
6.7* ☎624/104–3274 ═MC, V.

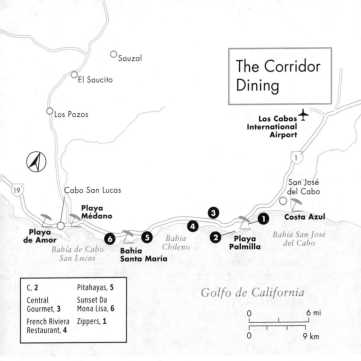

The Corridor Dining

Los Cabos International Airport

Cabo San Lucas

Playa Médano

Playa de Amor

Bahía de Cabo San Lucas

Bahía Santa María

Bahía Chileno

Playa Palmilla

Costa Azul

San José del Cabo

Bahía San José del Cabo

Golfo de California

C, 2	Pitahayas, 5
Central Gourmet, 3	Sunset Da Mona Lisa, 6
French Riviera Restaurant, 4	Zippers, 1

0 ———— 6 mi
0 ———— 9 km

¢–$$ ✕**Zippers.** Home to the surfing crowd and those who don't mind a bit of sand in their burgers, this casual palapa-roof restaurant is on Costa Azul beach just south of San José. Casual doesn't begin to describe the crowd, which can get downright raunchy. It's fine for young kids in the daytime; they'll enjoy running from the dining table to the sand. Sporting events sometimes blare on the TV. ⊠*Carretera 1, Km 18.5* ☎*624/172–6162* ▭No credit cards.

ASIAN

★ Fodor'sChoice ✕**Pitahayas.** In this elegant niche above the
$$$–$$$$ beach at Cabo del Sol, chef Volker Romeike blends Thai, Polynesian, and Chinese ingredients. He matches lobster with a vanilla-bean sauce, scallops with a sweet chili glaze, and the catch of the day with a Thai curry sauce. Soft jazz plays in the background, and the service is impeccable. Dress to impress. ⊠*Sheraton Hacienda del Mar, Carretera 1, Km 10* ☎*624/145–8000* ▭AE, MC, V.

CLOSE UP

Dining In

Eating every meal in a Los Cabos restaurant can devour your dollars quickly. Most food and liquor is shipped from the mainland or imported from the United States, resulting in premium prices. Many hotel rooms have small refrigerators and coffeemakers; some have microwaves, too. By stocking up on groceries you can save your money for splurges.

Supermarkets such as Cabo San Lucas's **Aramburo** (⊠*Av. Cárdenas across from Hard Rock Cafe, Cabo San Lucas* ☎*624/143–1450*), open 7 AM– 11 PM, and neighborhood markets sell the basics for quick meals. Watch out for the prices on imported goods—a box of

imported cereal can cost $5 or more. Stick with Mexican brands. Prices are lower at **ISSSTE** (⊠*Av. de la Juventud and Morelos, Cabo San Lucas* ☎*624/143–4658*). It's open 8–8. Inventory is limited, how-ever, and no meat or produce is sold. A good strategy is to get what you can at ISSSTE, then tap the smaller markets away from touristy areas. At **Costco** (⊠*Hwy. 1, Km 4.5* ☎*624/146–7180*), members can stock up on inexpensive supplies. For liquor in particu-lar, stock up at the airport's duty-free shop at your depar-ture airport. Liquor stores are generally less expensive than supermarkets and stay open until 11 PM (earlier on Sunday).

FRENCH

$$$–$$$$ **French Riviera Restaurant.** Master chef of France Jacques
★ Chretien at the helm of his own open kitchen and views of the Sea of Cortez and El Arco—it doesn't get more fabulous than this. You might find yourself as delightedly confounded as we were deciding what to watch. Earth tones and low-slung wicker chairs offset the white table-clothed tables, lending a cozy vibe to the sophisticated spot. Though the menu changes every three months, look for braised red snapper with provencal gratin potatoes and zucchini in a basil reduction. Finish with melted chocolate cake with pear puree or strawberries Napo-leon. ⊠*Carretera 1, Km 6.3* ☎*624/142–3350* ⊕*www. frenchrivieraloscabos.com* ⊟*MC, V.*

ITALIAN

$$–$$$ ×**Sunset Da Mona Lisa Italian Restaurant.** Cocktail tables along the cliffs have full-on views of El Arco, making this the best place to toast the sunset before moving to the candlelt din-ing room. Lobster pasta, crab with garlic and olive oil, and

Cabo San Lucas Dining	
Capo San Giovannis, 12	
Edith's Restaurant, 15	
Fish House, 6	
El Galeón, 1	
Gordo's Tortas, 9	
Lorenzillo's, 13	
Mama's Royal Cafe/Felix, 8	
Marisquería Mazatlán, 16	
Mi Casa, 10	
Misiones de Kino, 11	
Mocambo, 17	
Nick San, 5	
The Office, 14	
Pancho's, 3	
Sancho Panza, 4	
Sea Queen, 2	
Señor Greenberg's Mexicatessen, 7	

pasta with anchovies and capers are all great choices. Dinner reservations are essential at this romantic spot, which is sometimes taken over by wedding parties. ⊠*Carretera 1, Km 5.5* ☎*624/145–8160* ⊘*No lunch* ⊟*MC, V.*

CABO SAN LUCAS

Cabo San Lucas is *in*—especially for its rowdy nightlife and slew of trendy restaurants. A pedestrian walkway lined with restaurants, bars, and shops anchored by the sleek Puerto Paraíso mall curves around Cabo San Lucas harbor, itself packed with yachts. The most popular restaurants, clubs, and shops are along Avenida Cárdenas (the extension of Highway 1 from the Corridor) and Boulevard Marina, paralleling the waterfront.

AMERICAN

¢–$ ✕ **Señor Greenberg's Mexicatessen.** Pastrami, chopped liver, knishes, bagels, lox, cheesecake—you can find them all behind the glass counters of this decent Mexican incarnation of a New York deli. It's open 24 hours; the air-conditioning, stacks of newspapers, and soft music might pull you back more than once. There's a second location in Puerto Paraíso, with a huge dining room and a patio. Look for the new Señor Greenberg's in the Puerto Paraíso shopping mall overlooking the marina. ⊠*Plaza Nautica on Blvd. Marina, Centro* ☎*624/143–7808 or 624/144-3804* ▭*MC, V.*

ECLECTIC

★ **Fodor's**Choice ✕**Nick San.** Owner Angel Carbajal is an art-
$$–$$$$ ist behind the sushi counter (and also has his own fishing boats that collect fish each day). A creative fusion of Japanese and Mexican cuisines truly sets his masterpieces apart. The sauce on the cilantro sashimi is so divine that diners sneak in bread to sop up the sauce with (rice isn't the same). You can run up a stiff tab ordering sushi. The mahogany bar and minimalist dining room are packed most nights, but the vibe is upbeat, and many diners eat here so frequently they've become friends. There's a branch in the Corridor at Central Gourmet. Reservations are recommended. ⊠*Blvd. Marina, next to El Tesoro, Centro* ☎*624/143–4484* ⊕*www.nicksan.com* ▭*MC, V.*

$–$$$ ✕**El Galeón.** Considered by some the most distinguished dining room in town, El Galeón serves traditional Italian, Mexican, and American fare. Dishes are expertly prepared, with an emphasis on thick, tender cuts of beef. The choice seats look out to the marina, and the heavy wooden furnishings and white linens lend a sense of formality. Stop into the piano bar for a late-night brandy. ⊠*Across from marina by the road to Finisterra Hotel* ☎*624/143–0443* ▭*AE, MC, V.*

$–$$$ ✕**The Office.** Playa Médano is lined with cafés on the sand, some with lounge chairs, others with more formal settings. The Office, with its huge sign (the perfect photo backdrop), is the best. Cold beer, ceviche, nachos, fish tacos, french fries, and burgers are served in portions that somewhat justify the high prices. You can split most entrées. Dinners of grilled shrimp, fish with garlic, and steaks are popular; reservations are a must. ⊠*Playa Médano, Playa Médano* ☎*624/143–3464* ▭*MC, V.*

ITALIAN

$–$$$ ✕**Capo San Giovannis.** The sound of sauces simmering in the open kitchen blends with strains of opera at this intimate Italian restaurant. Owner Gianfranco Zappata, and his wife and master pastry chef, Antonella, perform a culinary concert that keeps you coming back for encores. Try their green salad with lobster chunks, cioppino Calabrese, spaghetti with crab, and *mela* (an apple-and-nut pastry topped with caramel). For a romantic touch, dine on the starlit back patio. There's a 10% discount for cash. ✉*Guerrero at Av. Cárdenas* ☎624/143–0593 ▭MC, V ⊗*Closed Mon.*

MEDITERRANEAN

$$–$$$ ✕**Sancho Panza.** The classy menu, decor, and live Latin rhythms make this small bistro a favorite with sophisticates. Try the steamed mussels, osso buco, and chicken with sun-dried apricots and walnuts. The menu changes constantly, as does the art in the Dalíesque bar. ✉*Blvd. Marina, behind KFC, Centro* ☎624/143–3212 ▭AE, MC, V ⊗*No lunch.*

MEXICAN

$$–$$$ ✕**Mi Casa.** One of Cabo's best restaurants is in a cobalt-blue building painted with a mural of a burro. The fresh tuna and dorado, served with tomatillo salsa or Yucatecan achiote, both shine, as does the sophisticated poblano *chiles en nogada* (stuffed with a meat-and-fruit mixture and covered with white walnut sauce and pomegranate seeds). The large back courtyard glows with candlelight at night, and mariachis provide suitable entertainment. The owners operate several excellent area restaurants, including Mi Casa de Mariscos and Peacocks. ✉*Av. Cabo San Lucas, Centro* ☎624/143–1933 ⊕*www.micasa.name* ▭MC, V.

$$–$$$ ✕**Pancho's.** Owner John Bragg has an enormous collection of tequilas, and an encyclopedic knowledge of the stuff. Sample one or two of the 500 labels and you'll truly appreciate the Oaxacan tablecloths, murals, painted chairs, and streamers more than you did when you first arrived. Try regional specialties like tortilla soup or chiles rellenos. The breakfast and lunch specials are a bargain. ✉*Hidalgo, between Zapata and Serdan, Centro* ☎624/143–2891 ⊕*www.panchos.com* ▭AE, MC, V.

$–$$ ✕**Misiones de Kino.** You may feel like you've discovered a well-kept secret when you enter this palapa-roofed house with adobe walls a few blocks off the main strip. Sit on the front patio or in a backyard hut hung with weathered old lanterns and photographs of the Mexican Revolution. Menu highlights are *cabrilla con salsa de frambuesa* (sea bass with raspberry sauce), *camarón coco* (coconut shrimp with mango sauce), and the crab or fish with garlic sauce. A second menu, called Pasta Bella, offers a wide range of pastas and Italian dishes. ✉*Guerrero and 5 de*

Mayo ☎624/105–1418 ▭*No credit cards* ⊘*Closed Sun. No lunch.*

¢–$$ ✕**Mama's Royal Cafe/Felix.** Mama's serves up bountiful breakfasts of omelets, poached eggs with avocado and ham, and cream cheese-stuffed French toast topped with bananas and pecans. The fried potatoes are superb. At night, the colorful restaurant becomes Felix, serving chiles en nogada, *pozole* (pork soup with hominy, onion, garlic, dried chilies, and cilantro), and other Mexican specialties along with a lineup of unusual salsas (the owner is a salsa pro). ⊠*Hidalgo at Zapata* ☎624/143–4290 ▭*MC, V.*

¢ ✕**Gordo's Tortas.** Listen for the blaring Beatles' tunes to find Gordo's tiny sidewalk stand. His tacos and *tortas* (sandwiches) are made with loving care, and his fans are loyal enough to chow down on their feet as there are only two small plastic tables by the stand. You can have two or three ham and cheese tortas for the price of one elsewhere. ⊠*Guerrero at Zapata, Centro* ☎*No phone* ▭*No credit cards.*

SEAFOOD

$$–$$$$ ✕**Edith's Restaurant.** The Caesar salad and flambéed crepes ☏ are prepared table-side at this small café, where dinners are accompanied by Mexican trios or soft jazz. Even the simplest choices are enhanced: quesadillas have Oaxacan cheese and homemade tortillas, and meat and fish dishes are given unusual chili or tropical fruit sauces. Families dine in early evening, so come in later if you're looking for a romantic atmosphere. ⊠*Paseo del Pescador, near Playa Médano* ☎624/143–0801 ⊕*www.edithscabo.com* ▭*MC, V* ⊘*No lunch.*

$$–$$$$ ✕**Lorenzillo's.** Gleaming hardwood floors and polished brass give a nautical flair to this dining room, where fresh lobster is king. Lorenzillo's has long been a fixture in Cancún, where lobster is raised on the company's farm. That Caribbean lobster is shipped to Los Cabos and served 12 ways (the simpler preparations—steamed or grilled with lots of melted butter—are best). It's a major splurge: a two-pounder served with spinach puree and linguine or potato sets you back over $66. Other options—coconut shrimp or beef medallions—are more moderately priced. ⊠*Cárdenas at Marina, Centro* ☎624/105–0212 ⊕*www.lorenzillos. com.mx* ▭*AE, MC, V.*

$$$$–$$$$ ✕**Mocambo.** Veracruz—a region known for its seafood preparations—meets Los Cabos in an enormous dining room packed with locals. The menu has such hard-to-find regional dishes as octopus ceviche, shrimp empanadas, and a heaping mixed seafood platter that includes sea snails, clams, and octopus, with lobster and shrimp. Musicians stroll among the tables and the chatter is somewhat cacophonous, but you're sure to have a great dining experience here. ✉*Leona Vicario at Calle 20 de Noviembre, Centro* ☎624/143–2122 ⊟MC, V.

$$$ ✕**Sea Queen.** A coffee and dessert bar sits beside the ☺ entrance to this enormous palapa-covered restaurant with playground equipment for kids to one side, a sushi bar, and a lounge area. Despite the overwhelming size of the place, the service is attentive, and the chef adds a regional flair to his fish dishes by fixing them with poblano, guajillo, or chipotle chilies or *damiana*, a local liqueur. The Mexican combo plate or Thai chicken salad should satisfy those who shun fish. ✉*Av. Cabo San Lucas at Blvd. Marina, Centro* ☎624/144–4731 ⊟MC, V.

$–$$ ✕**Fish House.** Walk up the stairs to this glassed-in terrace restaurant and leave the noisy bars and marina action behind. Courteous waters bustle between tables spread with green cloths, serving tuna carpaccio, scallop ceviche, and spicy calamari salad. Fried chicken and other meat dishes are available for dedicated carnivores, but why not try dorado or snapper fresh from the sea? ✉*Blvd. Marina at Plaza de la Danza* ☎624/144–4501 ⊟MC, V.

★ Fodor'sChoice ✕**Marisquería Mazatlán.** The crowds of locals
¢–$$ lunching at this simple seafood restaurant are a good sign—as are the huge glasses packed with shrimp, ceviche, and other seafood cocktails. You can dine inexpensively on wonderful seafood soup, or spend a bit more for tender *pulpo ajillo* (marinated octopus with garlic, chilies, onion, and celery). ✉*Mendoza at Calle 16 de Septiembre, Centro* ☎624/143–8565 ⊟MC, V.

Budget Bites

You can dine reasonably in Los Cabos if you're not scared by the myth that the food at mom-and-pop operations or at street stands will send you running for the bathroom. These places usually cook to order, so you can tell if something has been sitting out too long or hasn't been cooked well. If there's a crowd of locals, the food is probably fresh and well prepared. Safe bets include quesadillas, fish tacos, corn on the cob, and *tortas* (sandwiches). Some restaurants have a *comida corrida* (prepared lunch special), a three-course meal that consists of soup or salad, an entrée with rice and vegetables, coffee, and a small dessert. It's not gourmet, but you'll be sated economically.

In Cabo San Lucas, head for the taco stands behind Squid Roe and Avenida Cárdenas and the backstreets inland from the marina. **Carnitas El Michoacano** (⊠ *Vicario between Carranza and Obregón, Cabo San Lucas*) sells savory roasted pork served in tacos or tortas for about $3 each. At **Pollo de Oro** (⊠ *Morelos, at Av. Cárdenas, Cabo San Lucas*), plus

other locations, a half-chicken meal costs about $5.

For inexpensive Mexican eateries close to the marina and hotels, try the juice stands. **Rico Suave** (⊠ *Cardenas between Hidalgo and Guerrero, Cabo San Lucas*) makes great smoothies with yogurt, as well as cheese tortas. **Oye Como Va** (⊠ *Guerrero and Zapata, Cabo San Lucas*), a juice stand, also serves *molletes* (sliced rolls with beans and cheese) for $1.50. **Cafe Europa** (⊠ *Blvd. Marina, Cabo San Lucas*) has a big breakfast burrito for $5 and quesadillas for $1.50.

In San José del Cabo, there are at least a dozen stands at the **Mercado Municipal.** You may be the only gringo at the tables—a great way to practice your Spanish. Stock up on fresh papayas, mangos, melons, and other peelable fruits. Look for reasonably priced restaurants on Zaragoza and Doblado by the market. Good taco stands line streets on the inland side of Highway 1. **Super Tacos Indios** has filling baked potatoes. **Las Ranas,** a *taquería* (taco eatery), has a full bar.

Where to Stay

WORD OF MOUTH

"Just a general comment...the Cabo San Lucas area has, percentage-wise, far fewer [all-inclusive] resorts than other popular Mexican beach resorts, so you may find your choices pretty limited if you insist on going AI."

—Bill_H

Updated
by Dan
Millington

SPRAWLING MEXICAN- and Mediterranean-style resorts dominate Los Cabos, especially along the Corridor. Hotel developments have gobbled up most of San Lucas's waterfront, and the amount of ongoing construction is astonishing. For years building restrictions have been threatened—or promised, depending on your view—but development continues.

Several megadevelopments in the Corridor contain two or more hotels, along with golf courses and private villas, and guests rarely leave the property. San José has large all-inclusive and time-share properties along the beach. Some small hotels and bed-and-breakfasts lie in or near town centers, and others are more remote. Very few are beachfront, but great deals, friendly service, and character make these inns popular. For high-season stays, try to make reservations at least three months in advance, and six months in advance for holidays. Precious few lodgings serve travelers on a budget.

Note that time-share representatives at the airport and in many hotel lobbies will try to entice you to attend a presentation by offering free transportation, breakfast, or activities. Don't feel obligated to accept—they often last at least two hours. If you're staying in a hotel that has time-share units, aggressive salespeople may call your room every morning asking you to attend a free breakfast. If you're not interested, demand to be taken off their call list.

ABOUT THE HOTELS

Bargains here are few and far between, and rooms at resort hotels generally start at $200 a night. For groups of six or more planning an extended stay, condos are a convenient and economical option. Otherwise, the best deals can be found at small bed-and-breakfasts, which are not plentiful and are usually booked early. You can find lower prices during off-season weeks—but don't expect huge discounts in Los Cabos.

We always list the facilities that are available, but we don't specify whether they cost extra; when pricing accommodations, always ask what's included and what costs extra.

Hotel rates in Baja California Sur are subject to a 10% value-added tax and a 2% hotel tax for tourism promotion. Service charges (at least 10%) and meals generally aren't included in hotel rates. Several of the high-end properties include a daily service charge in your bill; be sure you know the policy before tipping (though additional tips for extra service are always welcome). The Mexican government categorizes hotels, based on qualitative evaluations, into *gran turismo* (superdeluxe, or six-star, properties, of which there are only about 50 nationwide); five-star down to one-star; and economy class.

Assume that hotels operate on the European Plan (EP, with no meals) unless we specify that they offer a Continental Plan (CP, with a Continental breakfast), Breakfast Plan (BP, with a full breakfast), Modified American Plan (MAP, with breakfast and dinner), or the Full American Plan (FAP, with all meals). Hotels in this guide have air-conditioning and private bathrooms with showers unless stated otherwise.

4

WHAT IT COSTS IN U.S. DOLLARS				
HOTELS				
$$$$	$$$	$$	$	¢
over $250	$150–$250	$75–$150	$50–$75	under $50

Hotel prices are for two people in a double room in high season.

SAN JOSÉ DEL CABO

San José's downtown is lovely, with adobe houses and jacaranda trees. Entrepreneurs have converted old homes into stylish restaurants and shops, and the government has enlarged and beautified the main plaza. An ambitious multiyear beautification process is underway. Backers hope to get streets repaved, buildings remodeled, and parks installed. A nine-hole golf course and residential community are south of Centro (town center); farther south the ever-expanding Zona Hotelera (hotel zone) faces a long beach on the Sea of Cortez.

★ Fodor'sChoice   ☒ **Casa Natalia.** A graceful boutique hotel,
$$$$ Casa Natalia is on San José's most charming street. Rooms are done in regional Mexican motifs and have soft robes, king-size beds, remote-control air-conditioning, and private patios screened by bamboo and bougainvillea. Suites have hot tubs and hammocks on large terraces. A free shuttle takes you to a beach club in the Corridor. The restaurant, Mi Cocina, is fabulous. Staffers are help-

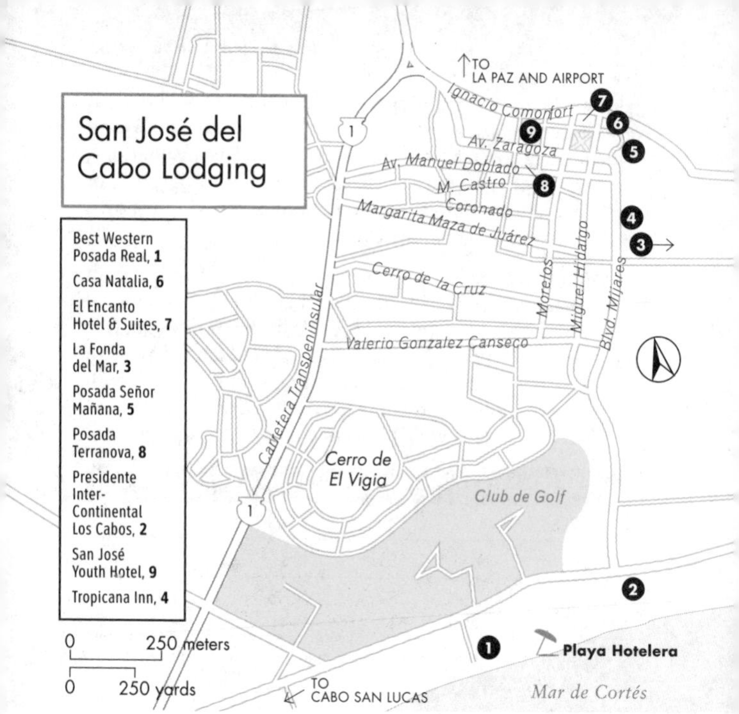
San José del Cabo Lodging
Best Western Posada Real, 1
Casa Natalia, 6
El Encanto Hotel & Suites, 7
La Fonda del Mar, 3
Posada Señor Mañana, 5
Posada Terranova, 8
Presidente Inter-Continental Los Cabos, 2
San José Youth Hotel, 9
Tropicana Inn, 4
TO LA PAZ AND AIRPORT
Ignacio Comonfort
Av. Zaragoza
Av. Manuel Doblado
M. Castro
Coronado
Margarita Maza de Juárez
Cerro de la Cruz
Valerio Gonzalez Canseco
Morelos
Miguel Hidalgo
Blvd. Mijares
Carretera Transpeninsular
Cerro de El Vigia
Club de Golf
Playa Hotelera
Mar de Cortés
TO CABO SAN LUCAS
0 250 meters
0 250 yards

ful and welcoming. (Families take note: children under 13 aren't allowed.) ✉*Blvd. Mijares 4, Centro, 23400* ☎*624/146–7100, 888/277–3814 in U.S.* 🌐*www.casanatalia.com* *14 rooms, 2 suites* *In-room: safe. In-hotel: restaurant, bar, pool, concierge, laundry service, no elevator* ▭*AE, MC, V* *CP.*

$$$$ **Presidente InterContinental Los Cabos.** Cactus gardens surround this low-lying hotel, one of the originals in what's become a lineup of massive all-inclusives. There's a friendly, old-world Mexican attitude among the staff members, many of whom have been here for decades. Each of the hotel's three sections is centered by pools and lounging areas. Ground-floor rooms, which have terraces, are the best. All rooms have showers but no bathtubs. The quietest rooms were once next to the estuary, but noise from construction on the nearby Puerto los Cabos development can now be a problem. As a result of the hurricane that slammed the southern tip of Baja in 2006, the Presidente has gone through extensive renovations. Operations are now back to normal. The excellent Da Antonio Italian restaurant isn't part of the all-inclusive plan, but a stay here does get you a discount. ✉*Paseo San José, at end of hotel*

Cabo Condos

CLOSE UP

If you're planning to stay a week or more, renting a condo can be much more economical and convenient than staying in a hotel. Los Cabos has countless condominium properties, ranging from modest to ultra-luxurious. Many private owners rent out their condos, either through the development's rental pool or property management companies. The price is the same for both, but with the latter you might get a better selection.

Nearly all condos are furnished and have a fully equipped kitchen, a television, bed and bath linens, laundry facilities, and maid service. Most are seaside and range from stu-

dios to three bedroom units. Though a minimum stay of one week is typically required, some condominiums require even longer stays. Start the process at least four months in advance, especially for high-season rentals. **Cabo Homes and Condos** (☎624/142–6244 ☒624/142–6245 ⊕www.cabohomesandcondos. com) handles a large number of vacation rentals. **Cabo Villas** (☎800/745–2226 in U.S. and Canada, 831/475–4800 elsewhere ☒831/475–4890 ⊕www.cabovillas.com) represents several properties including the high-end homes at Villas del Mar in the One&Only Palmilla compound.

zone, Zona Hotelera, 23400 ☎624/142–0211, 800/424–6835 in U.S. ⊕www.ichotelsgroup.com ⇋395 rooms, 7 suites ⌂In-room: safe, dial-up. In-hotel: 6 restaurants, room service, bars, tennis courts, pools, gym, beachfront, children's programs (ages 5–12), laundry service, no-smoking rooms ⊟AE, MC, V ⏀AI.

$$$ ☒**Best Western Posada Real.** One of the best values in the hotel zone, this beachside property consists of two tri-level, Santa Fe–style buildings. Every room has a balcony and at least a partial ocean view, a bathtub and shower, and a refrigerator. The large heated pool has a palapa-roof swim-up bar. The hotel is quiet compared to its all-inclusive neighbors and frequently draws business travelers. ☒Malecón, Zona Hotelera, 23400 ☎624/142–0155, 800/528–1234 in U.S. ☒624/142–0460 ⊕www.posadareal.com.mx ⇋140 rooms, 8 suites ⌂In-room: safe, dial-up. In-hotel: 2 restaurants, room service, bars, tennis courts, pool, beachfront, laundry service, public Internet, no elevator ⊟AE, MC, V.

$$ 🖭 **El Encanto Hotel & Suites.** Located near many great restaurants, this inn has two buildings—one with standard rooms and a second across the street with suites, some of which have kitchens and patios. All guest quarters are immaculate, and both buildings are surrounded by gardens. The suite building has a gallery and a poolside restaurant. ⊠ *Morelos 133, Centro, 23400* ☎ *624/142–0388* ⊕ *www.elencantoinn.com* ⤙ *12 rooms, 14 suites* ⌂ *In-room: kitchen (some). In-hotel: pool, laundry service, no elevator* ⊟ *AE, MC, V* ⏣ *EP.*

$$ 🖭 **La Fonda del Mar.** If you're looking for a peaceful retreat, this hotel on a long secluded beach fits the bill. And once the diners clear out of the popular Buzzard's Bar & Grill it's even more tranquil. The three thatch-roof cabañas and one suite are in heavy demand in high season. The whole operation runs on solar power. Cabañas have in-suite toilets and sinks but share a hot-water shower; the suite has in-room facilities. To get here, turn off Boulevard Mijares at the signs for Puerto Los Cabos and follow the road up the hill past La Playa; it's about 10 minutes outside town. ⊠ *Old East Cape Rd., 23400* ☎ *624/113–6368 cell, 624/110–6454, 951/303–9384 in U.S.* ⊕ *www.vivacabo. com* ⤙ *3 cabañas, 1 suite* ⌂ *In-room: no a/c. In-hotel: restaurant, bar, beachfront, no elevator* ⊟ *No credit cards* ⏣ *Closed Aug.* ⏣ *BP.*

$$ 🖭 **Tropicana Inn.** This small hotel is great as long as you aren't desperate to be on the beach. The stucco buildings, which have tile murals of Diego Rivera paintings, frame a pool and palapa bar in a quiet enclave behind San José's main boulevard. Rooms are well maintained. ⊠ *Blvd. Mijares 30, Centro, 23400* ☎ *624/142–1580* ⊕ *www.tropicanacabo. com* ⤙ *39 rooms, 2 suites* ⌂ *In-room: refrigerator. In-hotel: restaurant, room service, bar, pool, gym, parking (no fee), no elevator* ⊟ *AE, MC, V* ⏣ *EP.*

$–$$ 🖭 **Posada Terranova.** People return to San José's best inexpensive hotel so frequently they almost become part of the family. The large rooms have two double beds and tile bathrooms. Whether you congregate with other guests at the front patio tables or in the restaurant, it still feels like a private home. ⊠ *Calle Degollado at Av. Zaragoza, Centro, 23400* ☎ *624/142–0534* ⊕ *www.hterranova.com.mx* ⤙ *25 rooms* ⌂ *In-hotel: restaurant, room service, bar, no elevator* ⊟ *AE, MC, V.*

¢–$ ☐**Posada Señor Mañana.** Accommodations at this friendly, eccentric place run the gamut from small no-frills rooms to larger rooms with air-conditioning, fans, cable TV, coffee-makers, and refrigerators. Hammocks hang on an upstairs deck, and you can store food and prepare meals in the communal kitchen. The owners also have inexpensive cabañas by the beach (see www.eldelfinblanco.net for further information on the cabañas). ✉*Obregón, by Casa de la Cultura, Centro, 23400* ☎*624/142–0462* ⊕*www.srmanana. com* ⏎*9 rooms, 1 suite* &*In-room: no a/c (some), no TV (some). In-hotel: no elevator* ☰*MC, V* ☉*CP.*

¢ ☐**San José Youth Hostel.** The rock-bottom conditions at this hostel don't discourage budget travelers who appreciate having a private bathroom for less than $10 per person for a double. Rooms vary from freshly painted to downright dreary; knowledge of Spanish helps when dealing with management and fellow guests. The market and the town's best taco stands are within easy walking distance. ✉*Obregón, between Guerrero and Calle Degollado, Centro, 23400* ☎*624/355–3310* ⏎*20 rooms* &*In-room: no a/c, no phone, no TV, no elevator* ☰*No credit cards.*

THE CORRIDOR

Even before the Corridor had an official name and a paved road, the hotels here were expensive and exclusive, with private airstrips. Little has changed, and developers have deliberately kept it high-end. It's the most valuable strip of real estate in the region, with golf courses, luxury developments, and unsurpassed views of the Sea of Cortez.

$$$$ ☐**Cabo Surf Hotel.** Legendary and amateur surfers alike claim the prime break-view rooms at this small hotel in the cliffs above Playa Costa Azul. They mingle by the horizon swimming pool and in the cozy restaurant (which is a great place to enjoy a wonderful meal and stunning views), and they schedule their day's activities around the wave action. Rooms are spacious enough for two wave-hounds to spread out their gear; some have French doors that open to the sea breezes. Book early at this popular spot. ✉*Hwy. 1, Km 28, 23410* ☎*624/142–2666, 858/964–5117 in U.S.* ⊕*www.cabosurfhotel.com* ⏎*22 rooms* &*In-room: kitchen (some). In-hotel: restaurant, bar, pool, public Wi-Fi, no elevator* ☰*MC, V.*

The Corridor Lodging

Sauzal

El Saucito

Los Pozos

Cabo San Lucas

San José del Cabo

Playa Médano

Costa Azul

Playa de Amor

Bahía San José del Cabo

Bahía de Cabo San Lucas

Bahía Santa María

Bahía Chileno

Playa Palmilla

Golfo de California

⑧ ⑥ ⑤ ④ ⑦ ③ ② ⑩ ⑨ ①

Cabo Surf Hotel, **1**	Misiones del Cabo, **9**	Twin Dolphin, **7**
Casa del Mar Beach, Golf & Spa Resort, **5**	One&Only Palmilla, **2**	Las Ventanas al Paraíso, **6**
Esperanza, **10**	Sheraton Hacienda del Mar Resort, **8**	Westin Resort & Spa, Los Cabos, **3**
Marquis Los Cabos, **4**		

0 ————— 6 mi
0 ————— 9 km

★ **Fodor'sChoice** 🏨 **Casa del Mar Beach, Golf & Spa Resort.** It's all
$$$$ about comfort and privacy at this hacienda-style hotel.
A hand-carved door leads into the courtyard-lobby, and
stairways curve up to the rooms, spa, and library. Guest
quarters have bathrooms with whirlpool bathtubs a few
steps above the main bedroom. A series of streams, fountains, and gardens leads around the pool to a wide stretch
of beach and a beach club restaurant. ⊠*Carretera 1, Km
19.5, 23410* 🖀*624/145–7700, 888/227–9621 in U.S.*
⊕*www.casadelmarmexico.com* 🛏*56 suites* 🖧*In-room:
safe, dial-up. In-hotel: 2 restaurants, room service, bars,
tennis courts, pools, gym, spa, beachfront, concierge,
laundry service* ⊟*AE, MC, V.*

★ **Fodor'sChoice** 🏨 **Esperanza.** It's an utterly polished inn with
$$$$ a focus on privacy. The smallest suite is 925 square feet.
Some suites are right on a secluded beach; all have handcrafted furnishings, Frette linens, and dual-head showers. Villas take the luxe even further with private pools
and butler service. Californian and Mexican recipes get a
Baja twist in the restaurant. At the spa you can relax with
a stone massage or bask in a steam cave. ⊠*Carretera 1,
Km 3.5, 23410* 🖀*624/145–6400, 866/311–2226 in U.S.*

⊕*www.esperanzaresort.com* ➤*50 casita suites, 6 luxury suites* ⌂*In-room: safe, DVD, Wi-Fi. In-hotel: 3 restaurants, room service, pool, gym, spa, beachfront, concierge, laundry service, no elevator* ⊟*AE, MC, V.*

★ Fodor'sChoice 🖫**Marquis Los Cabos.** Stunning architecture,
$$$$ attention to detail, and loads of luxurious touches make the Marquis a standout. Suites have Bulgari toiletries, reversible mattresses (hard or soft), high-speed Internet connections, and original art. Casitas also have private pools and refrigerators and are right on the beach. The serpentine swimming pool curves along the edge of the sand, beneath waterfalls. Food is excellent and reasonably priced. ⊠*Carretera 1, Km 21.5, 23410* ☎*624/144–2000, 877/238–9399 in U.S.* ⊕*www.marquisloscabos.com* ➤*216 suites, 28 casitas* ⌂*In-room: safe, dial-up, Wi-Fi, refrigerator. In-hotel: 3 restaurants, room service, bar, pool, gym, spa, beachfront, executive floor, no-smoking rooms* ⊟*AE, MC, V* ⊚*CP.*

$$$$ 🖫**One &Only Palmilla.** This world-class resort has a spa,
★ a Charlie Trotter restaurant, and a Jack Nicklaus golf course. Two pools seem to flow over low cliffs to the sea. Hand-painted tiles edge stairways leading to rooms and suites, where beds are overloaded with pillows, bathtubs are deep, and water in the shower truly rains down upon you. Your quarters also have Bose sound systems, flat-screen TVs, and wireless Internet access. Some patios and terraces have daybeds and straight-on sea views. ⊠*Carretera 1, Km 27.5, 23400* ☎*624/146–7000, 800/637–2226 in U.S.* ⊕*www.oneandonlyresorts.com* ➤*61 rooms, 91 junior suites, 20 1-bedroom suites* ⌂*In-room: safe, DVD, dial-up, Wi-Fi, refrigerator. In-hotel: 2 restaurants, room service, bars, golf course, tennis courts, pools, gym, spa, beachfront, water sports, concierge, laundry service, no-smoking rooms* ⊟*AE, MC, V.*

$$$$ 🖫**Sheraton Hacienda del Mar Resort.** Small tile domes painted
☾ red, orange, and pink top eight buildings at this majestic resort. Rooms have white walls, cobalt textiles, and terracotta-tile floors; whirlpool tubs and large balconies with ocean views take the hotel beyond chain standards. The 450-yard beach is beautiful to stroll on, and sometimes the sea is calm enough for a swim. A small beach just to the south is sheltered by rocky points. ⊠*Carretera 1, Km 10, 23410* ☎*624/145–5800, 888/672–7137 in U.S.* ⊕*www.sheratonhaciendadelmar.com* ➤*270 rooms, 31 suites* ⌂*In-room: safe, kitchen (some), dial-up, refrigera-*

Pamper Parlors

Los Cabos is nirvana for spa-lovers. Most spas in the high-end resorts are open to the public, and all offer massage treatments, from Swedish, deep-tissue, and sports to aromatherapy, shiatsu, and various forms of reflexology in the spa. Other high-demand services are body scrubs and wraps, in which sea salts, volcanic clay, seaweed, chamomile, or other natural elements exfoliate the skin and improve circulation. Cleansing, revitalizing facials are often used to treat wrinkles, acne, and sunburns.

Consistently rated one of the top spas in the world, **Las Ventanas al Paraíso Spa** (⊠*Hwy. 1, Km 19.5* ☎*624/144–0300* ⊕*www. lasventanas.com/spa.cfm*) is a must for any spa addict. The rates for treatments are only slightly higher than at other area spas, yet the eclectic specialties range from ayurvedic body treatments and Indonesian traditional rituals, to ancient Tepezcohuite and Nopal (Mexican) healing wraps. **Esperanza** (⊠*Hwy. 1, Km 3.5* ☎*624/145–8641* ⊕*www. esperanzaresort.com*) has a soothing full-service spa where guests are greeted with a choice of *aguas frescas* (fruit juices with water). To complete the pampering, waterfall showers and soaks in rock-enclosed

hot tubs are available before and after treatments. Guests receive their treatments in private villas with hot tubs and sun beds at the Mandara Spa in the **One&Only Palmilla** (⊠*Hwy. 1, Km 7.5* ☎*624/146–7000* ⊕*www.one-andonlypalmilla.com*). The spa at the **Westin Resort & Spa Los Cabos** (⊠*Hwy. 1, Km 22.5* ☎*624/142–9001* ⊕*www.star-wood.com/westin*) is notable for its well-regarded therapists and its adjoining fitness center. Check out the reproductions of Baja's cave paintings at **Villa del Palmar Spa** (⊠*Old Road to San José, Km 0.5* ☎*624/143–4460*). **Pueblo Bonito Rosé Spa** (⊠*Playa Médano* ☎*624/143–5500* ⊕*www.pueblobonito.com*) is an elaborate affair with a Roman bath motif.

Spa packages combining three or four services can be relatively economical, although most still exceed $200. Nearly all spas also offer haircuts, manicures, pedicures, and waxing services. Many offer free use of fitness facilities—hot tub, steam room, sauna, and exercise equipment—with a spa treatment; otherwise, they may charge $15 to $25. No matter which spa you choose, make a reservation at least one day in advance.

tors (some). In-hotel: 4 restaurants, room service, bars, pools, gym, spa, beachfront, children's programs (ages 5– 12), laundry service, public Internet, no-smoking rooms ⊟*AE, DC, MC, V.*

$$$$ ☐**Twin Dolphin** Sleek and Japanese-modern, the Twin Dolphin has been a hideaway for the rich and famous since 1977 and has a loyal following of guests seeking seclusion. The minimalist rooms are in low-lying casitas along a seaside cliff. The hotel is worth a visit just to see the reproductions of Baja cave paintings on the lobby wall. Meal plans are available for an additional fee. ⊠*Carretera 1, Km 11.5, 23410* ☎*624/145–8190, 800/421–8925 in U.S.* ⊟*624/143–0496* ⊕*www.twindolphin.com* ⇌*44 rooms, 6 suites* ⏃*In-room: no phone, safe, refrigerator, no TV. In-hotel: restaurant, bar, tennis courts, pool, beachfront, laundry service, no-smoking rooms, no elevator* ⊟*AE, MC, V.*

★ Fodor'sChoice   ☐**Las Ventanas al Paraíso.** Despite the high room
$$$$ rates at this ultraprivate pleasure palace, it's often hard to get a reservation. Guests luxuriate in suites with hot tubs, fireplaces, and telescopes for viewing whales or stars. Newer hotels have copied such Ventanas-style touches as handcrafted lamps and doors, inlaid stone floors, and tequila service, but the originator is still the best. Service is sublime, the restaurants are outstanding, and the spa treatments reflect the latest trends. The three spa suites have private spa butlers and in-suite treatments. There's a minimum night stay for weekends depending on the season. ⊠*Carretera 1, Km 19.5, 23400* ☎*624/144–2800, 888/767–3966 in U.S.* ⊕*www.lasventanas.com* ⇌*68 suites, 3 spa suites* ⏃*In-room: safe, VCR, dial-up, refrigerator. In-hotel: 3 restaurants, room service, bar, tennis courts, pools, gym, spa, beachfront, water sports, laundry service, no-smoking rooms, some pets allowed, no elevator* ⊟*AE, MC, V* ⏅*EP, FAP, MAP.*

$$$$ ☐**Westin Resort & Spa, Los Cabos.** The architecturally
★   astounding Westin is a magnificent conglomeration of colors, shapes, and views. The rooms, set above a man-made beach, are among the best in this price range and have Westin's trademark "Heavenly Beds," with cushy pillows and comforters. Villas have full kitchens and whirlpool tubs that face the sea. The hotel has so many amenities, including a fabulous spa and gym, you may never need to leave the grounds. It's a long walk from the parking lot and lobby to the rooms and pools, though. ⊠*Hwy. 1, Km 22.5,*

4

23400 ☎624/142–9000, 888/625–5144 in U.S. ⊕www.
starwood.com/westin ☞243 rooms &In-room: safe, refrigerator (some). In-hotel: 5 restaurants, room service, 4 bars,
2 tennis courts, 7 pools, gym, spa, beachfront, concierge,
children's programs (ages 5–12), laundry service, no-smoking rooms ☱AE, MC, V.

$–$$ ▣ **Misiones del Cabo.** Some of the condos at this unpreten-
tious complex have balconies with a hot tub and spectacular views of El Arco. Six beige Santa Fe–style buildings on a
secluded beach house the condos, most of which have one
or two bedrooms, though some are studios (the two-bed-
rooms run up to $315 per night). A free hotel shuttle runs
back and forth to nearby San Lucas. Surfers enjoy the prox-
imity to Monumentos, a great left break. ⊠Carretera 1,
Km 5.5, 23400 ☎624/145–8090 ☎624/145–8097 ⊕www.
misionescabo.com ☞42 condos &In-room: kitchen, VCR.
In-hotel: restaurant, tennis courts, pool, laundry service,
no-smoking rooms ☱AE, MC, V.

CABO SAN LUCAS

In Cabo San Lucas there's a massive hotel on every available plot of waterfront turf. A pedestrian walkway lined
with restaurants, bars, and shops anchored by the sleek
Puerto Paraíso mall curves around Cabo San Lucas harbor,
itself packed with yachts. Unfortunately, a five-story hotel
complex at the edge of the harbor blocks the water view
and sea breezes from the town's side streets, which are filled
with a jarring jumble of structures. The short Pacific coast
beach in downtown San Lucas is more peaceful, though
humongous hotels have gobbled up much of the sand. An
entire new tourism area dubbed Cabo Pacifica by developers has blossomed on the Pacific, west of downtown.

$$$$ ▣ **Pacifica Holistic Retreat & Spa.** Soothing waterfalls, glass-
dome ceilings, and pebbled floors bring nature indoors
to complement the holistic approach to vacationing. The
emphasis here is on health and wellness; a physician who
works with natural therapies oversees the Armonia spa,
where treatments include watsu and a temezcal. Rooms
have minimalist decor with cream fabrics, cedar and straw
accents, and stunning ocean views. The designers incorpo-
rated Feng Shui elements throughout the resort. ⊠Cabo
Pacifica s/n ☎624/142–9696 or 866/585–1752 ⊕www.
pueblobonitopacifica.com ☞154 rooms &In-room: safe,

Cabo San Lucas Lodging

Ethernet, Wi-Fi, refrigerator. In-hotel: 2 restaurants, room service, 2 bars, 2 pools, gym, spa, beachfront, laundry service, public Internet ≡AE, MC, V.

$$$–$$$$ 🏊 **Marina Fiesta.** Though this colonial-style building is not ocean-side, most rooms have a pleasant view of the cloverleaf-shape pool and the yacht-filled marina just below. Rooms are designed for practicality, with stain-proof floral textiles, tile floors, and plenty of space to spread your stuff about. The hotel is on the walkway around the marina, next to popular bars and shops and a five-minute walk from Playa Médano. ⊠*Marina, Lot 37, Marina, 23410* ☎*624/145–6020* ⊕*www.marinafiestaresort.com* 🛏*139 rooms, 46 suites* ♿*In-room: safe, kitchen (some), refrigerator (some). In-hotel: restaurant, room service, bar, pools, gym, spa, laundry service, public Internet, public Wi-Fi* ≡AE, MC, V.

$$$–$$$$ 🏊 **ME Cabo** The most popular beach in Los Cabos is where you'll find the ME—Sol Melia's entrée into the personality-driven W-style hotel brand—and its huge, bustling pool areas, hot tub under the palms, and all the equipment you could need for playing on, and in, the water. Rooms have

easygoing light-wood furnishings and heavy drapes to block out the midday sun; you'll even find an iPod docking station and plasma TV. Early reservations are essential. ✉*Playa Médano, 23410* ☎*624/145–7800, 800/336–3542 in U.S.* 🖶*624/143–0420* 🌐*www.mebymelia.com* ⬒*144 rooms, 6 suites* &*In-room: safe, Wi-Fi. In-hotel: 3 restaurants, pools, beachfront, laundry service* ⊟*AE, MC, V.*

$$$–$$$$ 🏨**Solmar Suites.** One of the first San Lucas hotels, the Solmar sits against the rocks at land's end facing the Pacific. Rooms are done in a Mexico–Santa Fe style, with subdued green- and blue-tile baths. The oldest rooms open right to the sand. Newer buildings run up a tiered hillside; it's a hike to the beach and pools. Time-share units (also used as hotel rooms) have kitchenettes and a private pool area. The surf here is far too dangerous for swimming, but don't miss a stroll along the wide strip of beach. The Solmar's sport-fishing fleet is first-rate. The restaurant hosts a Saturday night Mexican fiesta; the food in the bar is better. ✉*Av. Solmar at Blvd. Marina, Apdo. 8, Pacific Coast, 23410* ☎*624/146–7700, 310/459–9861, 800/344–3349 in U.S.* 🌐*www.solmar.com* ⬒*82 junior suites, 14 studios, 27 deluxe suites* &*In-room: safe, refrigerator. In-hotel: restaurant, room service, bar, pools, beachfront, laundry service* ⊟*MC, V.*

$$$ 🏨**Pueblo Bonito Rosé.** Mediterranean-style buildings curve
☾   around elegant grounds, imitations of Roman busts guard reflecting pools, and Flemish tapestries adorn the lobby. Not your typical Cabo hotel, but this company never goes half-way. There are two Pueblo Bonito hotels in San Lucas and two on the Pacific coast. A shuttle bus travels between them and guests have signing privileges at all four. Even the Rosé's smallest suites can accommodate four people, and all have private balconies overlooking the grounds. (Many suites are time-share units; the salespeople are sometimes very aggressive—stand your ground.) ✉*Playa Médano, 23410* ☎*624/142–9898, 800/990–8250 in U.S.* 🌐*www. pueblobonito.com* ⬒*260 suites* &*In-room: safe, kitchen, refrigerator. In-hotel: 2 restaurants, room service, bars, pools, gym, spa, beachfront, laundry service, public Internet* ⊟*AE, MC, V.*

$$$ 🏨**Villa del Palmar.** Both time-share and hotel guests appre-
☾   ciate the large rooms with kitchenettes and an array of amenities at this ever-growing property a five-minute walk north of Playa Médano. The whale-shape waterslide at

the three-level pool shows that families are welcome. The aroma of bread and pizzas baking in the wood-burning oven wafts from the first-rate open-air restaurant. Elegant condolike units are also available at the adjacent Villa la Estancia complex of private villas; rates for a one-bedroom villa start at $365. ⊠*Camino Viejo a San José, Km 0.5, 23410* ☎*624/145–7000* 📠*624/143–2664, 877/845–5247 in U.S.* ⊕*www.villadelpalmarloscabos.com* ⊋*457 suites, 96 villas* ⚲*In-room: safe, kitchen (some), VCR, dial-up. In-hotel: 2 restaurants, room service, bars, pools, gym, spa, children's programs (ages 4–12), laundry service, public Internet* ⊟*MC, V.*

$$–$$$ 🗆**The Bungalows Hotel.** If solitude and a reasonable room rate are more important than being in the center of the action, this is your place. In several two-story buildings that frame a small, heated pool, the rooms are smartly decorated with Mexican textiles and art. It's about 10 blocks from the beach. ⊠*Blvd. Miguel Angel Herrera, 5 blocks from main plaza, 23410* ☎*888/424–2252 in U.S.* 📠*624/143–5035* ⊕*www.cabobungalows.com* ⊋*16 suites* ⚲*In-room: kitchen (some), VCR, DVD. In-hotel: pool, no-smoking rooms, public Wi-Fi, no elevator* ⊟*MC, V* ⊺❙*BP.*

$$–$$$ 🗆**Casa Bella.** The Ungson family had been in Cabo for more than four decades before turning their home across from Plaza San Lucas into an inn. It's the classiest place in the neighborhood, landscaped with paths leading to a pool and terrace. Room furnishings are handcrafted and thoughtfully arranged. Open showers in the huge tiled bathrooms are works of art—some even have little gardens. The property feels totally secluded, though it's in the middle of town. ⊠*Calle Hidalgo 10, Centro, 23410* ☎*624/143–6400* ✐*hotelboutiquecb@yahoo.com* ⊋*7 rooms, 1 suite* ⚲*In-room: no TV. In-hotel: pool, laundry service, no-smoking rooms, no elevator* ⊟*MC, V* ⊗*Closed Aug. and Sept.* ⊺❙*CP.*

$$–$$$ 🗆**Finisterra.** One of the oldest hotels in Cabo, the Finisterra is also one of the most modern, with two towers that rise directly from the beach. An eight-story palapa covers the restaurant and bar on the beach next to two free-form swimming pools. Rooms in the new buildings are by far the nicest and have oceanfront balconies. The stone buildings of the less-expensive older section of the hotel evoke fishing lodges. The restaurant is good, and the Whale Watcher

bar atop a high cliff has the best view in town. ⊠*Blvd. Marina, 23410* ☎*624/143–3333, 800/347–2252 in U.S.* 🖷*624/143–0590* ⊕*www.finisterra.com* ⚓*287 rooms* ⚐*In-room: kitchen (some). In-hotel: 2 restaurants, bars, tennis courts, pools, spa, beachfront, concierge, refrigerator, public Internet, public Wi-Fi* ⊟*AE, MC, V.*

$$–$$$ 🖳**Marina Sol Condominiums.** Good bargains can be found here—especially for groups of three to six people. Most of the condos are two-bedroom, but some have one, three, or five bedrooms. Only a few blocks from the town center and Playa Médano, this is a good spot if you like being close to the action. Reserve at least three months in advance for high season. Try to negotiate better rates for long-term stays. ⊠*Paseo del Pescador, 23410* ☎*624/143–3231 or 877/255–1721* 🖷*624/143–6286* ⊕*www.marinasolresort. com* ⚓*52 condos* ⚐*In-room: kitchen (some), refrigerator, VCR (some). In-hotel: restaurant, bar, pool, laundry service, public Wi-Fi, public Internet* ⊟*MC, V.*

$–$$ 🖳**Los Milagros.** A mosaic sign (made by co-owner Ricardo
★   Rode) near the entrance hints at the beauty inside this small inn. Brilliant purple bougainvillea and orange lipstick vines line the patio, which showcases more of Rode's works by the fountain and small pool. *Bóveda*-style (arched brick) roofs top the rooms, which have terra-cotta-tile floors and handmade Guadalajaran furniture. One room is accessible to travelers with disabilities. Owner Sandra Scandiber dispenses budget travel tips while visiting with guests in the courtyard, and is always ready to lend books from her huge library. Checks or cash are accepted at the hotel; to use a credit card, you must pay prior to arrival through PayPal. ⊠*Matamoros 116, Centro, 23410* ☎*718/928–6647 in U.S.* ☎🖷*624/143–4566* ⊕*www.losmilagros.com. mx* ⚓*12 rooms* ⚐*In-room: kitchen (some). In-hotel: pool, laundry service, public Internet, public Wi-Fi, no elevator* ⊟*AE, D, MC, V.*

$ 🖳**Cabo Inn.** The small, comfortable rooms at this palapa-roof hotel have tangerine and cobalt sponge-painted walls and stained-glass windows above the headboards. The eight rooms on the lower level have refrigerators; a kitchen, barbecue and picnic area, small pool, and a television round out the communal amenities. ⊠*Calle 20 de Noviembre and Vicario, Centro, 23410* ☎🖷*624/143–0819, 619/819–2727 in U.S.* ⊕*www.caboinnhotel.com* ⚓*20 rooms* ⚐*In-room: refrigerator, no TV. In-hotel: no elevator* ⊟*MC, V.*

$ ⊠**Hotel Santa Fe.** There's a friendly, make-yourself-at-home feeling at this small hotel that resembles a two-story apartment building. Room service is provided by the deli at the adjacent market. Large rooms have sofa beds and cable TV. The beach is a 10-minute walk away and the pool isn't heated. Ask about deals for weekly stays. ⊠*Av. Zaragoza and Obregón, 23410* ☎*624/143–4401* ☎*624/143–4402* ⊠*46 rooms* ⚘*In-room: kitchen. In-hotel: room service, pool, laundry facilities, laundry service, no elevator* ⊟*MC, V.*

$ ⊠**Siesta Suites.** The proprietors keep a close eye on this three-story hotel—a calm refuge two blocks from the marina—and they offer great budget tips. The suites have full-size refrigerators, and between the bedrooms with two double beds and living rooms with wide padded couches that make excellent beds even for grown-ups, there's room to sleep quite a crew. Internet is available in the lobby. ⊠*Calle Zapata, Apdo. 310, Centro, 23410* ☎*624/143–2773, 866/271–0952 in U.S.* ⊕*www.cabosiestasuites.com* ⊠*5 rooms, 15 suites* ⚘*In-room: kitchen. In-hotel: pool, no elevator* ⊟*MC, V.*

¢–$ ⊠**Club Cabo Hotel, RV Park & Campground.** Though only a five-minute drive from Playa Médano, this small complex is quiet and remote. It sits amid dense vegetation between the beach and Highway 1 and has tent and RV camping alongside well-maintained motel rooms and a long pool. Parking is secure and prices very reasonable. Reservations are accepted for rooms but not for the RV/tent sites. ⊠*Off Old Road to San José, Km 3, just east of Villa del Palmar, 23410* ☎*624/143–3348* ⊕*www.mexonline.com/club-cabo.htm* ⊠*10 rooms, 18 tent/RV sites* ⚘*In-room: kitchen (some), refrigerator (some). In-hotel: pool, laundry facilities, public Internet, no elevator* ⊟*No credit cards.*

¢ ⊠**Hotel Melida.** This bare-bones hotel in a commercial neighborhood offers simple but immaculately clean rooms. The televisions are encased in metal cages, which make one wonder about the clientele. But the management is friendly and helpful, and you can walk to Playa Médano in about 15 minutes. It's a few blocks away from the bars by the marina, which may explain the precautions. Noise can be a problem. ⊠*Matamoros at Niños Héroes, 23410* ☎*624/143–6564* ⊠*14 rooms* ⚘*In-hotel: no elevator* ⊟*No credit cards.*

Nightlife
& the Arts

WORD OF MOUTH

"Downtown Cabo [San Lucas] is party central most of the year, so [if you are looking for a quiet vacation] maybe you are going to the wrong place."

—Bill_H

Updated
by Dan
Millington

PARTY-MINDED CROWDS roam the main strip of Cabo San Lucas every night from happy hour through late-night dancing—often staggering home or to their hotel rooms just before dawn. It's not hard to see why this is *the* nightlife capital of southern Baja. Indeed, San Lucas is internationally famous (or infamous, depending on your view) for being a raucous party town, especially during Spring Break. Most of the nightlife is focused on bars and dance clubs, where a very lively pickup scene predominates. Beware the tequila shooters and Jell-O shots forced upon revelers by merry waiters—they cost at least $5 each. Topless bars and "gentleman's" clubs are abundant, too. Single men are often accosted outside San Lucas bars with offers for drugs and sex, but beware—you could be falling into a police trap.

After-dark action in San José del Cabo caters mostly to locals and tourists seeking tranquillity and seclusion. What little nightlife there is revolves around restaurants, casual bars, and large hotels—coming to life on Thursday and going back to sleep Sunday. There are no big dance clubs or discos in San José (though in this fast-changing scene, something may open by the time you visit).

Between the two towns, the self-contained resorts along the Corridor have no nightlife to speak of. Only resort guests frequent the hotel bars, and the sunset-watching crowd departs soon after darkness descends. If you want to dance the night away, stay in Cabo San Lucas.

For years Todos Santos has been the bohemian center of southern Baja, and Los Cabos has concerned itself with partying. But Los Cabos now has a fledgling arts scene. A few galleries and talented artists in Cabo San Lucas brave the party scene and open studios. Some Los Cabos hotels hold special art events, during which prominent local artists, often with international reputations, exhibit their works and meet the public.

Cabo's first annual jazz festival was held in July 2003, and organizers say they will continue presenting the festival, though no dates are set. There's also a Baja Reggae Fest at San Pedrito (between Cabo San Lucas and Todos Santos) usually held in February.

Classical-music and dance performances remain few and far between. If you're looking for music, stop by the Puerto Paraíso mall in Cabo San Lucas starting around 5 PM or 7 PM,

Waking the Dead

Celebrated throughout Mexico, the most important religious and indigenous festival in Los Cabos takes place November 1 and 2: All Saints' and All Souls' Day, more commonly referred to as **Día de los Muertos** (Day of the Dead). Long before Spain conquered Mexico, the festival was part of Indian culture and held during the winter equinox. In true colonial spirit, Spain changed the timing to coincide with its religious All Saints' and All Souls' Day.

Not as macabre as it sounds, the festival is a joyous celebration to welcome a visit from the souls of deceased loved ones. Family and friends prepare favorite foods and drink of the dearly departed, burn candles and incense, and place flowers in cemeteries and at memorials along the road. Shops carry candy shaped like skulls and coffins, and bread is baked to look like ghosts. No tears are to be shed, as it is said that the path back to the living world must not be made slippery by tears.

when you might find folkloric dance performances by the marina or jazz concerts in the Japanese garden area. At the Solmar Suites hotel in Cabo San Lucas (☎624/146–7700), a Mexican Fiesta, with a buffet dinner, folkloric dance show, and games, is held every Saturday night. Fortunately there has been an increasing interest in the history and culture of Baja, which may lead to a richer artistic environment, with more events such as these, in the years to come.

ABOUT THE NIGHTLIFE

Bars and clubs in San José del Cabo and Cabo San Lucas don't usually have cover charges unless a well-known group is playing. Many don't even open until 10 PM. Closing times are determined by specific government licenses and vary greatly; the latest is 5:30 AM. The drinking age in Mexico is 18, but it's not strictly enforced.

For information about local happenings, check out the free English-language newspapers *Gringo Gazette* or *Destino: Los Cabos*. The English-Spanish *Los Cabos News* is also a good source for local events listings. These papers are available at most hotels and stores. Or, go to www.loscabosguide.com.

SAN JOSÉ DEL CABO

BARS

If you feel the need to belt out *Love Shack* or *My Way,* grab the karaoke mike at **Cactus Jack's** (⊠*Blvd. Mijares 88* ☎*624/142–5601*), a gringo hangout that's open until the wee hours on weekends.

The 18-hole miniature golf course at the **Rusty Putter** (⊠*Plaza Los Cabos, across from Fiesta Inn* ☎*624/142–4546*), an open-air sports bar, is its best feature. Long holes, creative obstacles, and variations in the carpet make it a particularly good course. The bar and course are open 8 AM–1 AM.

Tropicana Inn guests, other travelers, and locals thrilled to have a happening place to enjoy live music mingle at the **Tropicana Bar and Grill** (⊠*Blvd. Mijares 30* ☎*624/142–1580*). Conversation is usually possible on the balcony overlooking the bar and stage, though when a really hot band gets going you'll be too busy dancing to talk.

Shooters Sports Bar (⊠*Manuel Doblado at Mijares* ☎*624/146–9900*), on the rooftop at the Tulip Tree restaurant, shows sporting events on big screen TVs. It's open until everyone leaves.

Los Amigos Smokeshop and Cigar Bar (⊠*Calle Hidalgo 11* ☎*624/142–1138*) has a classy cigar bar in a century-old house. They serve espresso, fine tequilas, and single-malt Scotch to go with the imports from their humidor. Look for visiting celebs here.

WHERE IT'S AT You may have to walk a gauntlet of servers waving menus in your face, but the sidewalk bars along the marina between Plaza Bonita and Puerto Paraíso are great places to hang out at happy hour.

JAZZ & SALSA

At the hip club **Havanas** (⊠*Hwy. 1, Km 29* ☎*No phone*), owner Sheila Mihevic sings in an excellent jazz band that performs Wednesday through Friday. A six-piece salsa band delights locals and tourists of all ages on weekends. Though the crowd tends to be upscale, food and drink prices are reasonable. The open-air, second-level bar is filled with antiques from Cuba and some from an old saloon in Nevada. Havanas is closed Sunday and Monday.

MOVIES

At **Cinema Versailles** (⊠*Hwy. 1, Plaza Cabo Ley, San José del Cabo* ☎*624/142–3333*) admission is $3.50, but the selection of movies is generally three or four months behind what's showing in the United States. Movies run in two theaters, with the last feature starting around 11 PM.

CABO SAN LUCAS

BARS

Ronald Valentino plays everything from *My Way* to *Besame Mucho* at the piano at **El Galeón** (⊠*Blvd. Marina* ☎*624/143–0443*). The crowd is generally quiet, though inebriated fans sometimes inspire an impromptu karaoke session.

At **Havanas** (⊠*Carretera 1, Km 29* ☎*No phone*) the excellent jazz band of owner-singer Sheila Mihevic plays in the hip club Wednesday through Friday.

At the noisy, friendly **Latitude 22+** (⊠*Av. Cárdenas, next to Costco* ☎*624/143–1516*), the slogan is "No Bad Days." It's a long-standing place to down cold beers or shots of tequila and mingle with old and new friends. At this writing, owner Mike Grzanich had begun building an enormous restaurant and bar called the Roadhouse in the Corridor (Hwy. 1, Km. 4.5) and had put Latitude 22+ up for sale. Check the status before heading out.

Facing Boulevard Marina and the boats in the water, the aptly named **Margaritaville** (⊠*Blvd. Marina* ☎*624/143–0010*) serves frozen margaritas in fishbowl-size glasses at outdoor tables. It's also a restaurant, but there's better food around.

Miami meets Cabo at **Nikki Beach** (⊠*Hotel Meliá San Lucas, Playa Médano* ☎*624/145–7800*). With white gauze canopies shading plush white sunbeds and lounge chairs around swimming pools, the club would be the perfect setting for a music video. DJs spin world-beat music while waiters serve salmon and scallop carpaccio and cornmeal-crusted calamari to scantily dressed hipsters.

Local professionals unbutton their shirt collars and gossip over beers at **Nowhere Bar** (⊠*Blvd. Marina* ☎*624/143–4493*). Two-for-one drinks are a draw, as is the large dance floor. Sushi and tacos are served from adjacent businesses,

5

and bartenders hand out baskets of popcorn to keep the thirst level high.

A hot spot for listening to live music, playing pool or darts, and watching sports on big-screen TVs, **Tanga Tanga** (⊠*Blvd. Marina outside Tesoro Resort* ☎*624/144–4501*) has a bar outdoors and another (air-conditioned) one inside. Local reggae and rock groups play here most afternoons and nights.

La Varitas (⊠*Calle Gomez, behind Puerto Paraíso* ☎*624/143–9999*) is a branch of a La Paz rock club favored by young Mexicans. One of Cabo's most popular clubs, it hosts live music almost every night.

BETTING

At **Caliente Casino Real** (⊠*Blvd. Marina at Plaza Nautica* ☎*624/143–1934*), a gambling hall, restaurant, and bar, virtually any sporting event or horse race in the United States and Mexico is fair game. You can follow the results on one of more than 30 TVs. The bar, at the back of the smoky betting salon, is filled with red lounge chairs and black, fake marble tables. It's open 9 AM to midnight.

DANCE CLUBS

Again & Again (⊠*Av. Cárdenas between Leona Vicario and Morelos* ☎*624/143–6323*) is the most attractive club in town. Two levels with pillared balconies overlook the stage and dance floor. On Thursday, the live *banda* (band) music draws a large crowd. The music, born in the 1950s in Monterrey, is traditional and often slow, for dancing in pairs. On other nights, the music is a mix of dance styles, including salsa and merengue.

Giggling Marlin (⊠*Blvd. Marina* ☎*624/143–1182*) has been around forever, but its gimmicks remain popular, and it has retained its popularity over the years. Watch brave (and inebriated) souls be hoisted upside down at the mock fish-weighing scale or join in an impromptu moonwalk between tables. The age of the clientele varies, as does the music, but the dance floor is usually jammed. A nightly two-for-one drinks special packs 'em in 11 PM to 1 AM. The bartender may place a shot of tequila in front of you the minute you sit down—you'll pay at least $5 if you drink it.

★ If you have any religious sensitivity, moral convictions, or a heart condition, you may want to think twice before entering **Squid Roe** (⊠*Av. Cárdenas* ☎*624/143–1269*). Just about anything goes here: waiters dance and gyrate with female

Hagar's Hangout: Cabo Wabo

According to local lore, in the mid-1980s former Van Halen lead singer Sammy Hagar and a friend were walking along the beach in Cabo San Lucas when they passed a drunk man stumbling. Hagar remarked, "Hey, he's doing the Cabo Wabo." A few years later, in 1990, Hagar and the rest of Van Halen opened the bar called Cabo Wabo—establishing one of the premier stops on the Cabo party circuit. When the group broke up in 1996, all but Hagar sold their shares in the bar.

Mexican and American rock bands perform every night. Almost always packed, the place erupts when Hagar comes to play. When he's on tour, he may only make it to the club four or five times a year. Three of those visits fall on April 22 (the bar's anniversary), October 3–4 for the bar's MELT DOWN celebration, and October 7–13 (for Hagar's birthday celebra-

tion). When not on tour, Hagar hits Cabo Wabo up to 12 times a year. The dates are usually announced on the club's Web site, www.cabowabo.com.

Often accompanying Hagar are some of his rock-and-roll friends, who come to perform with him. These have included Chris Isaak, Kirk Hammett of Metallica, David Crosby, Slash, Rob Zombie, the Cult, and the Sex Pistols.

Easily seen from afar because of a lighthouse replica at the main entrance, the bar was designed by architect Marco Monroy. He built high, cavernous ceilings and painted the walls with zebra stripes and psychedelic neon patterns. Hagar liked Monroy's work so much that the design of the bar was replicated for his set on the "Red Voodoo" tour. The club has four pool tables and numerous bars, one hung with bras and panties donated over the years by female patrons.

patrons, roaming waitresses shove Jell-O shots down your throat, frat-boy wannabes attempt beer-chugging contests, scantily clad dancers undulate in a makeshift penitentiary. During Spring Break or high season, more than 5,000 revelers come here on any given night—many stay until the 3 AM closing time. Feeling out of place? Head for the second-floor balcony, where the scene is a bit less sexy.

A Shot of Tequila

What once was a drink of the poor Mexican farmer is now enjoyed by the international set and comes in nearly 1,000 varieties. Low-purity brands (like Cuervo Gold) that crowd shelves outside of Mexico have given tequila a reputation as a foul-tasting, noxious liquor. But aficionados compare a good tequila to fine cognac.

Tequila must contain at least 51% blue agave, a plant related to the lily. The best tequilas are 100% blue agave. Liquid is distilled from the sap of 7- to 10-year-old plants and fermented. Mezcal, a 100% blue agave cousin of tequila,
is a liquor born in Oaxaca that is occasionally bottled with a worm (a practice that likely began as a marketing ploy). If you buy tequila with a worm, it was probably bottled in the United States, and is probably not good-quality tequila.

Most tequila is made in the town of Tequila, near Guadalajara. Labels bearing *reposado* indicate up to a year of aging; *añejo*, from one to three years. The longer tequila ages, the smoother it tastes. Sample a few before you buy; you're allowed only one liter through U.S. Customs.

GAY BARS

The only gay bar in Cabo San Lucas is **Rainbow Bar** (⊠ *Blvd. Marina at Marina Cabo Plaza* ☎ *624/143–1455*). It's on the marina but away from the nightlife scene. The small, simple space has large mirrors on every wall, a tiny dance floor in the far corner, and two TVs that show music videos. It plays a good mix of English and Spanish music. The owner is American, but most of the patrons are Mexican men.

MOVIES

Cinema Paraíso (⊠ *Av. Cárdenas at Puerto Paraíso* ☎ *624/143–1515* ⊕ *www.cinemaparaiso.com.mx*) has 10 theaters, including a VIP screening room with reclining leather seats. First-run movies are shown in Spanish and English.

ROCK CLUBS

The latest U.S. rock plays over an excellent sound system at **Cabo Wabo** (⊠ *Calle Guerrero* ☎ *624/143–1188*), but the impromptu jam sessions with appearances by Sammy Hagar—an owner—and his many music-business friends are the real highlight.

With its '59 pink Cadillac jutting through the window and dozens of rock-and-roll albums and other memorabilia on the walls, **Hard Rock Cafe** (✉*Blvd. Marina across from Squid Roe* ☎*624/143–3779*) is a typical member of the chain. Live rock music starts at 10 every night. Thursday is ladies' night, when women drink free from 9 to 11.

WINE BARS

With 250 wines from all over the world, **Sancho Panza** (✉*Blvd. Marina behind the lighthouse and within the Tesoro Resort* ☎*624/143–3212* ⊕*www.sanchopanza.com*) has the best wine list in town. Live blues or jazz fills the small bar every night. Though on the pricey side, the food is highly recommended. The bar closes when it closes and is open every night.

5

Beaches &
Water Sports

WORD OF MOUTH

"We did a snorkle cruise [in Cabo San Lucas] with Pez Gato. Very nice. It was a catamaran and headed to Santa Maria Beach for snorkling. The water was COLD compared to Hawaii or the Carribean, but it was very fun. We saw a whale on the way over and spent about 1 hour at the cove. On the way back they served lunch and cocktails. The crew was also fun. Would highly recommend them."

—MichelleY

Updated
by Dan
Millington

LONG STRETCHES OF COASTLINE along the Sea of Cortez and the Pacific Ocean allow for plenty of fun in the sand and surf. Add to that nearly 360 warm and sunny days per year, and you get a natural wonderland where outdoor activities can be enjoyed year-round. During winter, tourists from the north flock to this sun-licked playground to soak up the rays and challenge the waves. In the summer, tourists and locals alike head to the water for a break from the intense heat.

From crowded people-watching beaches to secluded coves, high-speed Jet Ski rides to leisurely fishing trips, and daring deep-sea scuba expeditions to casual snorkeling, the waters off Cabo offer endless possibilities.

ABOUT THE BEACHES
Most beaches in the area stay mob-free. The exception is Playa Médano, which is alongside Cabo San Lucas. Most people on this beach, however, are searching for crowds. None of the other beaches are within walking distance of either Cabo San Lucas or San José del Cabo; some can be accessed by boat, but most require a car ride (unless you're staying at a Corridor hotel nearby). You can reach nearly all the beaches by bus, but it may take a while. None of the beaches charges an admission fee.

BEACHES

Beneath the rocky cliffs of the Pacific Ocean and the Sea of Cortez lie many bays, coves, and unprotected swaths of sandy beach. The waters range from translucent green to deep navy, from calm to turbulent. Playa Médano, in Cabo San Lucas, is the most visited and active stretch of sand. Gorgeous and somewhat secluded Playa del Amor (Lover's Beach) is five minutes across the bay by water taxi. Just southwest of San José, the most popular beaches are Costa Azul and Playa Palmilla.

BEACHES NEAR SAN JOSÉ DEL CABO

Oh, the madness of it all. Here you are in a beach destination with gorgeous weather and miles of clear blue water, yet you dare not dive into the sea. Most of San José's hotels line **Playa Hotelera** on Paseo Malecón San José, and brochures and Web sites gleefully mention beach access. Although the long, level stretch of coarse brown sand is beautiful, the current is dangerously rough, and the drop-offs are steep and close to shore. Swimming here is extremely dangerous, and signs warn against it all along the way. Feel free to walk along the beach to the Estero San José, or play volleyball on the sand. But for swimming, head to Playa Palmilla in the Corridor.

BEACHES IN THE CORRIDOR

The Corridor's coastline edges the Sea of Cortez, with long secluded stretches of sand, tranquil bays, golf fairways, and hotel beaches. Few areas are safe for swimming. Some hotels have man-made rocky breakwaters that create semi-safe swimming areas when the sea is calm. As a rule, the turnoffs for the beaches aren't well marked. Facilities are extremely limited; lifeguards and public restrooms are nonexistent. △ **The four-lane Highway 1 has well-marked turnoffs for hotels, but it's not well lighted at night. Drivers tend to speed down hills, tempting vigilant traffic officers. Slow buses and trucks seem to appear from nowhere, and confused tourists switch lanes with abandon. Wait until you're safely parked to take in Sea of Cortez views.**

Bahía Santa María and Bahía Chileno are two beautiful strands in the Corridor. But for some truly secluded gems, drive an hour or two north of either town. Perhaps the most stunning and desolate beaches in the area are in Cabo Pulmo, one and a half hours north of San José or two hours from Cabo San Lucas.

★ **Bahía Chileno.** A private enclave—with golf courses and residences—is being developed at Bahía Chileno, roughly midway between San José and San Lucas. The beach skirts a small, crescent-shape cove with aquamarine waters that are perfect for snorkeling and swimming. At this writing, the dirt access road and parking lot were open, but time will tell how the developers will handle public access—required by law—to the bay. Ideal for swimming and snorkeling, this pretty Corridor beach skirts a small, crescent-shape cove with aquamarine water. On the western end stands a rocky cliff where the Hotel Cabo San Lucas is perched. Along the eastern edge, some 200 yards away, are boulders you can climb. On the trek down you may see some stray wrappers and cans, but the beach itself is clean and usually not too crowded. During winter, this part of the Sea of Cortez gets chilly—refreshing for a dip, but most snorkelers cut their swims short.

6

CLOSE UP

Surf's Up

The tip of Baja is rife with surfing spots—no secret to the hordes of wave riders who swarm here year-round. Right breaks dominate, but left breaks can be found at La Bocana (just outside San José del Cabo) and Playa Monumentos (the Corridor, near Misiones del Cabo Hotel).

At La Bocana, a freshwater estuary, giant tubes are created when heavy rains open the river mouth. Monumentos has consistently gut-wrenching waves. Little-known Nueve Palmas (Nine Palms), halfway between San José del Cabo and

Cabo Pulmo, has a right break perfect for long-boarders.

In summer, Costa Azul is the beach of choice; its world-famous, experts-only Zippers break often tops 12 feet. Next-best is Shipwrecks on the East Cape, about a half hour north of San José by car. In winter, surfers in the know head to the Pacific side to Los Cerritos, near Todos Santos. The large waves and expansive, rockless beach are ideal. Wherever you go, be respectful of local surfers, who know these waters well.

The only business on the beach is **Cabo Acuadeportes** (☎624/143–0117), which rents snorkel equipment and offers scuba diving and snorkeling trips to nearby sites; hours are erratic. The turnoff for the beach is near the Hotel Cabo San Lucas, Km 14.5 on the Transpeninsular Highway (Hwy. 1). There's a sign; from San José turn immediately after the hotel; from San Lucas, just before. ✉ *16 km (9 mi) west of San José del Cabo, 16 km (9 mi) east of Cabo San Lucas.*

☺ **Fodor's**Choice★ **Bahía Santa María.** Sometimes it feels like the vultures overhead are just waiting for your parched body to drop during the 10-minute walk from the parking lot to Bahía Santa María, a turquoise bay backed by cliffs and lined by a wide, sloping beach. Shade is nonexistent unless you sit in the shadows at the base of the cliffs. The bay, part of an underwater reserve, is a great place to snorkel: brightly colored fish swarm through chunks of white coral and golden sea fans. In high season there's usually someone renting snorkeling gear for $10 a day or selling sarongs, straw hats, and soft drinks. It's best to bring your own supplies, though, including lots of drinking water, snacks, and sunscreen. Snorkel and booze-cruise boats from San

Lucas visit the bay in mid-morning. Come in mid-afternoon for a Robinson Crusoe feel. A parking lot just off the highway is usually guarded; be sure to tip the guard. The bay is roughly 19 km (11 mi) west of San José and 13 km (8 mi) east of San Lucas. Turn off the highway's east side just north of the Twin Dolphin hotel, at the sign that reads ACCESSO A ZONA FEDERAL (Access to Federal Zone). ✉ *19 km (11 mi) west of San José del Cabo, 13 km (8 mi) east of Cabo San Lucas.*

Playa Costa Azul. Cabo's best surfing beach runs 3 km (2 mi) south from San José's hotel zone along Highway 1. Its Zippers and La Roca breaks (the point where the wave crests and breaks) are world famous. Surfers gather here year-round, but most come in summer, when waves are largest. Several condo complexes line the beach, which is popular with joggers and walkers. Swimming isn't advised unless the waves are small and you're a good swimmer. The turnoff to this beach is sudden; it's on the highway's east side, at Zippers restaurant, which is on the sand by the surf breaks. ✉ *Just southwest of San José.*

Playa Las Viudas (Twin Dolphin Beach). Beneath the Twin Dolphin Hotel, this small public beach is great for snorkeling (bring your own gear). Low tides reveal great tidal pools filled with anemone, starfish, and other sea creatures. Take the access road directly south of the hotel. ✉ *Hwy. 1, Km 12, the Corridor.*

Playa Palmilla. Check out the villas on the road to Playa Palmilla, the best swimming beach near San José. The entrance is from the side road through the ritzy Palmilla development; turn off before you reach the guard house at the star-studded One&Only Hotel Palmilla. There are signs, but they're not exactly large. The beach is protected by a rocky point, and the water is almost always calm. A few palapas on the sand provide shade; there are trash cans but no restrooms. Panga fishermen have long used this beach as a base, and they're still here, despite the swanky neighbors to the south. Guards patrol the beach fronting the hotel, discouraging nonguests from entering. ✉ *Entrance on Hwy. 1, at Km 27, 8 km (5 mi) southwest of San José del Cabo, the Corridor.*

BEACHES IN CABO SAN LUCAS

Fodor'sChoice★ **Playa del Amor.** Lovers have little chance of finding romantic solitude at Lover's Beach. The azure cove on the Sea of Cortez at the very tip of the peninsula may well be the area's most frequently photographed patch of sand. It's a must-see on every first-timer's list. Water taxis, glass-bottom boats, kayaks, and Jet Skis all make the short trip from Playa Médano to this small beach backed by cliffs streaked white with pelican and seagull guano. Snorkeling around the base of these rocks is fun when the water's calm; you may spot striped sergeant majors and iridescent green and blue parrotfish. Seals hang out on the rocks at the base of the arch. Walk along the sand to the Pacific side to see pounding white surf; just don't dive into these rough waters.

Swimming and snorkeling are best on the Sea of Cortez, where the clear green, almost luminescent water is unquestionably the nicest in San Lucas. The Pacific side is too turbulent for swimming but ideal for relatively secluded sunbathing. Vendors are scarce, so bring your own snacks and plenty of water. The beach is crowded at times, but never like Playa Médano. To get here, take a five-minute water-taxi ride or a 15- to 20-minute glass-bottom boat tour. Opt for the latter if you want to photograph the Arch from the Pacific. Both leave from the Cabo San Lucas marina or Playa Médano every hour until 3 PM. Contact **Pisces Water Sports** (⊠*Playa Médano next to Pueblo Bonito Rosé hotel* ☎044–624/148–7530 *cell phone* 📠624/143–4883) for information about the glass-bottom boat tour. ⊠*Just outside Cabo San Lucas, at El Arco.*

☺ **Playa Médano.** Foamy plumes of water shoot from Jet Skis and WaveRunners buzzing through the water off Médano, a 3-km (2-mi) span of grainy tan sand that's always crowded. When cruise ships are in town it's mobbed. Bars and restaurants line the sand, waiters deliver ice buckets filled with beers to sunbathers in lounge chairs, and vendors offer everything from fake silver jewelry to henna tattoos. You can even have your hair braided into tiny cornrows or get a pedicure. Swimming areas are roped off to prevent accidents, and the water is calm enough for toddlers. Several hotels line Médano, which is just north of downtown off Paseo del Pescador. Construction is constant on nearby streets, and parking is virtually impossible. The most popular area is around several bar-restaurants, where beach chairs and tables are set up. This is a hot spot for people-watching (and for singles seeking to be doubles). Be prepared to deal with the many crafts vendors cruising the beach. They're generally not pushy, so a simple head shake will do. ⊠ *Paseo del Pescador, Cabo San Lucas.*

Playa Solmar. Huge waves crash onto the sand on the Pacific side of San Lucas. This wide, beautiful beach stretches from land's end north to the cliffs of El Pedregal, where mansions perch on steep cliffs. Swimming is impossible here because of the dangerous surf and undertow; stick to sunbathing and strolling. From December to March you can spot gray whales spouting just offshore; dolphins leap above the waves year-round. The beach is at the end of Avenida Solmar off Boulevard Marina. Four resorts— Solmar, Terrasol, Playa Grande, and Finisterra—are all on this beach, but guests tend to stick to the hotel pools. ⊠ *Blvd. Marina to hotel entrances, Cabo San Lucas.*

BEACHES FARTHER AFIELD

Playa Cerritos. This long, expansive beach on the Pacific Ocean is famous among surfers for breaking wonderful waves during winter. Even if you don't ride the waves, you can watch them crash along the shore. The vast, unspoiled beauty of this soft-sand beach makes a visit worthwhile. Swimming is not recommended because of the strong currents.

Most of the surfing crowd camps or stays in RVs near the beach. The fairly secluded area covers the basics with a few conveniences—including water, a small food stand, and a surf shop. The beach is 2½ km (1½ mi) from Highway 19, which connects Cabo San Lucas and Todos Santos. ⊠ *65 km (40 mi) north of Cabo San Lucas, 13 km (8 mi) south of Todos Santos.*

WATER SPORTS

Waterskiing, Jet Skiing, parasailing, and sailing are found almost exclusively at Playa Médano, where you can also go kayaking and boating. At least eight good scuba-diving sites are near Playa del Amor. Cabo Pulmo, which has the only coral reef in the Sea of Cortez, has even more. Snorkeling is also popular. Both the Sea of Cortez and the Pacific ensure great waves for year-round surfing. Still, in

Fishing for Dollars

The busiest time in Los Cabos is neither Christmas nor Spring Break but rather the last week of October—when the world's most prestigious marlin fishing tournament, the **Bisbee Black & Blue Jackpot Marlin Tournament,** takes place. More than 200 boat crews come from around the world in attempts to claim prizes totaling more than $1 million. Boats range from 28-foot skiffs to 100-foot (and larger) yachts. The only qualification necessary is the entry fee, which is more than $15,000.

Prizes are awarded to those who haul in the greatest size and quantity of blue and black marlins during the three-day tournament. In 2003, the prize for a 565-pound blue marlin was a record-breaking $1,165,230. Marlins under 500 pounds aren't even counted; the largest single catch ever weighed in at 1,080 pounds. Even with state-of-the-art equipment and perfect techniques, each marlin takes at least two hours to reel in. The especially large and feisty ones have had crews struggling for up to eight hours. Once caught, the marlins are either released or donated to onlookers at the dock.

this uncontested "Marlin Capital of the World," sportfishing is perhaps the most famous water sport.

FISHING

There are more than 800 species of fish in the waters off Los Cabos, and some anglers seem determined to catch them all. The most popular quarry are the huge blue, black, and striped marlin, which leap with glistening majesty in the sea. Anglers more interested in putting the catch-of-the-day on the table aim for dorado (also called mahimahi), tuna, and wahoo. Something's always biting, but the greatest diversity of species swim Cabo waters from June to November.

Fishing charters arranged through hotels or sportfishing companies include a captain and crew, tackle, bait, licenses, drinks, and sometimes lunch. Prices start at $375 per half-day for a 28-foot cruiser that can carry two or three passengers. A larger cruiser with a head (bathroom) and sunbathing space starts at about $500—from here, the sky's the limit. Private boats have air-conditioned staterooms, hot-water showers, full kitchens, and every other imaginable amenity. Pangas (small motorized skiffs) with a skipper rent for about $200 to $250 for six hours. They're most comfortable with one or two passengers. Companies typically try to help solo anglers hook up with a group to share a boat.

Vendors along the harbor-front in Cabo San Lucas offer all sorts of fishing options. To choose the best one for you, hang out at the harbor between 1 PM and 4 PM when the boats come in and ask the passengers about their experiences.

Anglers are strongly encouraged to release any fish they won't eat, rather than bring them in as trophies. Marlin are often hauled in to be weighed for photos and then discarded because the meat is not very tasty. The fish you bring in can be weighed and filleted at the docks, and vendors are available to take your catch away to be frozen, smoked, or canned. Most restaurants gladly prepare your catch any way you like. Nearly all boats leave from the Cabo San Lucas harbor, either from the sportfishing docks at the south end of the harbor or from behind the Plaza Las Glorias Hotel.

6

SAN JOSÉ DEL CABO
Most hotels in San José can arrange fishing trips. Until the Puerto Los Cabos marina north of San José is completed, you can only catch large sport-fishing boats out of the marina in Cabo San Lucas.

Fishing gear and line are available at **Deportiva Piscis Fishing Tackle Shop** (⊠*Calle Mauricio Castro, San José del Cabo ♣near Mercado Municipal* ☎624/142–0332). The *pangas* (small skiffs) of **Gordo Banks Pangas** (⊠*La Playa, near San José del Cabo* ☎624/142–1147, 800/408–1199 in U.S. ⊕*www.gordobanks.com*) are near some of the hottest fishing spots in the Sea of Cortez: the Outer and Inner Gordo Banks. The price for three anglers in a small *panga* runs from $200 to $240. Cruisers, which can accommodate four to six people, are available for $350 to $530 per day.

THE CORRIDOR
Some Corridor hotels have fishing fleets anchored at the Cabo San Lucas Marina; all can set up fishing trips. **Francisco's Fleet** (⊠*Playa Palmilla, the Corridor* ☎624/142–1092, 800//521–2281 in U.S.) has long been a favorite for its pangas with shade awnings and plastic seats. The outfitter

also has cruisers. **Victor's Sport Fishing** (☎624/122–1092)
has a fleet of pangas on the Palmilla resort's beach. Rates
start at $180.

CABO SAN LUCAS

The **Gaviota Fleet** (✉*Bahía Condo hotel, Playa Médano,
Cabo San Lucas* ☎624/143–0430 *or* 800/932–5599 @*www.
grupobahia.com*) currently holds the record for the largest
marlin caught in Cabo's waters. The company has charter
cruisers and pangas.

Jig Stop Tours (✉*34186 Coast Hwy., Dana Point, CA 92629*
☎*800/521–2281 in U.S.* @*www.jigstop.com*) books fishing trips for several Los Cabos fleets.

Renowned tackle store **Minerva's** (✉*Madero, between Blvd.
Marina and Guerrero, Cabo San Lucas* ☎624/143–1282
@*www.minervas.com*) has four charter-fishing boats.

At the long-established **Solmar Fleet** (✉*Blvd. Marina, Cabo
San Lucas* ✛*across from sport-fishing dock* ☎624/143–
0646, 624/143–4542, *or* 800/344–3349 @*www.solmar.
com*), boats and tackle are always in good shape, and regulars wouldn't fish with anyone else.

Some of the Corridor's priciest hotels choose the **Pisces
Sportfishing Fleet** (✉*Cabo Maritime Center, Blvd. Marina,
Cabo San Lucas* ☎624/143–1288 @*www.piscessportfish-
ing.com*). The fleet includes the usual 31-foot Bertrams,
plus 50- to 70-foot Hatteras cruisers with tuna towers
and staterooms.

JET SKIING & WATERSKIING

Several operators in Cabo San Lucas offer comparable, if
not identical, prices. Both Jet Skiing and waterskiing cost
about $45 for a half hour and $70 for a full hour.

JT Water Sports (✉*Playa Médano, Cabo San Lucas*
☎624/144–4566) has every type of water- and land-sports
equipment, including diving gear, WaveRunners, Windsurfers, and parasails. WaveRunners rent for $80 an hour;
parasailing costs $40. **Omega Sports** (✉*3 locations on Playa
Médano, Cabo San Lucas* ☎624/143–5519) offers Jet Skiing. **Pisces Watersports** (✉*Far side of Playa Médano, Cabo
San Lucas* ☎044–624/148–7530 *cell phone*) is a large
operation with Jet Skiing and waterskiing. It also rents
Hobie Cats by the hour, gives 12-minute rides on banana
boats (long, yellow inflatable rafts towed by high-speed

motorboats), and rents water-sports equipment. **Tío Sports** (⊠*Playa Médano, Cabo San Lucas* ⌖*by Meliá San Lucas* ☎624/143–3399) is a large operator with stands and offices throughout Los Cabos.

KAYAKING

The most popular and practical way to explore the pristine coves that dot the Los Cabos shoreline is by kayak. Day-long package tours that combine kayaking with snorkeling or scuba diving cost anywhere from $60 to $125. Single or double kayaks can be rented by the hour for $10 to $20.

SAN JOSÉ DEL CABO

In addition to the awesome beauty of the water, close-range views of a sea-lion colony attract kayakers to Cabo Pulmo.

For a combined kayak and snorkeling trip, try **Baja Salvaje** (⊠*Obregón at Guerrero, San José del Cabo* ☎624/148–2222 or 624/142–5300 ⊕*www.bajawild.com*), also called Wild Baja. Daylong trips include transportation, equipment, and lunch; you can substitute scuba diving for snorkeling. A full day tour costs $95.

If you have your own transportation to Cabo Pulmo, you can rent a kayak or take a trip with **Cabo Pulmo Beach Resort** (⊠*Hwy. 1 at La Ribera turnoff* ☎624/141–0244 ⊕*www. cabopulmo.com*). A six-hour guided tour to the sea-lion colony and environs includes lunch and snorkeling gear; tours depart at 9 AM.

Los Lobos del Mar (⊠*Brisas del Mar RV park, on south side of San José* ☎624/142–2983) rents kayaks and offers tours along the Corridor's peaceful bays. These outings are especially fun in winter when gray whales pass by offshore. Prices start at $30.

CABO SAN LUCAS

In Cabo San Lucas, Playa Médano is the beach to head for if you want to do some kayaking.

Omega Sports (⊠*Playa Médano* ☎624/143–5519) has good rates on single and double kayaks.

Cabo Acuadeportes (⊠*In front of the now-closed Hotel Hacienda, Playa Médano* ☎624/143–0117) has snorkeling and waterskiing, as well as good prices on kayak rentals.

An Underwater Paradise: Cabo Pulmo

One of Baja's true gems is Cabo Pulmo, the raw, un-spoiled national marine preserve along the Sea of Cortez. More than 5 mi of nearly deserted rocky beach border the only living coral-reef system on the Sea of Cortez. Several dive sites reveal hundreds of species of tropical fish, large schools of manta rays, and a sea-lion colony. This is a nearly perfect place for scuba diving and snorkeling.

The village of Cabo Pulmo has 100 or so residents, depending on the season. Power comes from solar panels, and drinking water is trucked in over dirt roads. Near the beach, solar-powered cottages are for rent at the **Cabo Pulmo Beach Resort** (⊠*Cabo Pulmo* ☎*624/141–0244* ⊕*www.cabopulmo.com*), which also has a full-service PADI dive facility. The town has two small general stores and three restaurants. Cabo Pulmo is a magnet for serious divers, kayakers, and windsurfers and remains one of southern Baja's natural treasures.

Tio Sports (⊠*Playa Médano* ☎*624/143–3399*) has kayak rentals and packages that include snorkeling.

JT Water Sports (⊠*Playa Médano* ☎*624/144–4566*) rents kayaks on the beach.

PARASAILING & SAILING

Parasailing costs between $30 and $40 for an eight-minute flight. Most operators won't tell you the stories about broken ropes, so proceed at your own risk. Sailboats and Windsurfers average about $20 per hour.

CABO SAN LUCAS

Cabo Acuadeportes (⊠*In front of now closed Hotel Hacienda, Playa Médano, Cabo San Lucas* ☎*624/143–0117* ⊠*Bahía Chileno, 16 km [9 mi] west of San José del Cabo, 16 km [9 mi] east of Cabo San Lucas*), one of the oldest operators in the area, rents Windsurfers and Sunfish sailboats. Both can be rented by the hour. This is the first shop on Playa Médano when coming from the Cabo San Lucas marina.

Parasails are among the many types of water-sports gear available at **JT Water Sports** (⊠*Playa Médano, Cabo San Lucas* ☎*624/144–4566*).

SCUBA DIVING

One of the pioneers of diving in the area was none other than Jacques Cousteau, who explored the **Sand Falls.** Only 150 feet off Playa del Amor, this underwater sand river cascades off a steep drop-off into a deep abyss. In fact, this is one of several excellent diving or snorkeling spots close to the Cabo San Lucas shore. There are also fantastic coral-reef sites in the Corridor and north of San José.

OPERATORS

All operators are based in Cabo San Lucas and offer essentially the same dives, at comparable prices. Generally, diving costs about $45 for one tank and $70 for two, including transportation. Equipment rental, dives in the Corridor, and night dives typically cost extra. Full-day trips to Gordo Banks and Cabo Pulmo cost about $125, including transportation, food, equipment, and two tanks. Most operators offer two- to four-day package deals.

Most dive shops have courses for noncertified divers; some may be offered through your hotel. Newly certified divers may go on local dives no more than 20 feet deep. Divers must show their C-card (diver certification card) before going on dives with reputable shops. Many operators offer widely recognized Professional Association of Diving Instructors (PADI) certification courses.

Amigos del Mar (⊠*Blvd. Marina, Cabo San Lucas ✛near harbor fishing docks* ☎*624/143–0505, 800/344-3349 in the U.S.* ⊕*www.amigosdelmar.com*) is the oldest and most complete dive shop in the Los Cabos area. The staff is courteous and knowledgeable, and all guides speak English.

Cabo Acuadeportes (⊠*In front of now closed Hotel Hacienda, Playa Médano, Cabo San Lucas* ☎*624/143–0117* ⊠*Bahía Chileno, 16 km [9 mi] west of San José del Cabo, 16 km [9 mi] east of Cabo San Lucas*) has boat dives from its shop on Playa Médano and boat and shore dives from its shop at Chileno Bay in the Corridor.

The *Solmar V* (⊠*Solmar Suites hotel, Blvd. Marina, Cabo San Lucas* ☎*624/143–0022, 310/455-3600 in U.S.* ⊕*www. solmar.com*), a luxury dive boat, takes weeklong trips to the islands of Socorro, San Benedicto, and Clarion, as well as to the coral reefs at Cabo Pulmo. Twelve cabins with private baths serve a maximum of 24 passengers.

6

DIVE SITES

At all of the sites in **Bahía San Lucas** near El Arco you're likely to see colorful tropical fish traveling confidently in large schools. Yellow angelfish, green and blue parrotfish, red snappers, perfectly camouflaged stonefish, and long, slender needlefish share these waters. Divers regularly encounter stingrays, manta rays, and moray eels. The only problem with this location is the amount of boat traffic. The sound of motors penetrates deep into the water and can slightly mar the experience. The **sea-lion colony** at Cabo Pulmo makes for a fun dive most of the year—except in summer, when these residents swim back out to sea. **Neptune's Fingers** (60–120 feet) is a long rock formation with abundant fish. About 150 feet off Playa del Amor, **Pelican Rock** (25–100 feet) is a calm, protected spot where you can look down on Sand Falls. **The Point** (15–80 feet) is a good spot for beginners who aren't ready to get too deep.

The Corridor has four popular diving sites. **Bahía Santa Maria** (20–60 feet) has water clear enough to see hard and soft corals, octopus, eels, and many tropical fish. **Chileno Reef** (10–80 feet) is a protected finger reef 1 km (½ mi) from Chileno Bay, with many invertebrates, including starfish, flower urchins, and hydroids. The **Blow-Hole** (60–100 feet) is known for diverse terrain—massive boulders, rugged tunnels, shallow caverns, and deep rock cuts—which house manta rays, sea turtles, and large schools of amberjacks and grouper. The **Shipwreck** (40–60 feet), an old Japanese fishing boat, is close to Cabo San Lucas, near the Misiones del Cabo hotel.

Three very unique diving spots can be found beyond the local area. The best spot for tropical fish and rays in the greater Los Cabos area is in the coral-reef system of the marine preserve at **Cabo Pulmo** (15–130 feet). The water is so clear that visibility can exceed 100 feet in summer. Expert divers head to **Gordo Banks** (100–130 feet), also known as the Wahoo Banks, which are 13 km (8 mi) off the coast of San José. The currents are too strong for less experienced divers. This is the spot for hammerhead sharks—not generally aggressive with divers—many species of tropical fish and rays, and, if you're lucky, dolphins. Fall is the best time to go. Well off the coast of **La Paz** (15–130 feet) you may find hammerhead and whale sharks.

SNORKELING

Many of the best dive spots are also good for snorkeling. Prime areas include the waters surrounding **Playa del Amor, Bahía Santa María, Bahía Chileno,** and **Cabo Pulmo.** Nearly all scuba operators also offer snorkel rentals and trips. Equipment rentals generally cost $10 per hour. Two-hour guided trips to Playa del Amor are about $25; day trips to Cabo Pulmo cost about $60. Most of the snorkeling and excursion boats are based in the Cabo San Lucas harbor.

BOAT TOURS

The most upscale boat in the Los Cabos area is a beautiful 48-foot catamaran called *La Princesa* (⊠*Cabo San Lucas Harbor, Cabo San Lucas* ☎*624/143–7676*). Daily trips to Bahía Santa María or Bahía Chileno depart between noon and 3 PM. For $49 per person, you get drinks, a light lunch, and equipment.

Oceanus (⊠*Blvd. Marina, Cabo San Lucas* ✢*by El Galeon restaurant* ☎*624/143–3929* ⊕*www.oceanusloscabos.com.mx*) leaves at 11 AM for snorkeling cruises.

Pez Gato (⊠*Plaza Las Glorias, Cabo San Lucas* ☎*624/143–3797* ⊕*www.pezgatocabo.com*) has several cruising options including a $49-per-person snorkeling trip.

Jungle Cruise (⊠*Plaza Las Glorias, Cabo San Lucas* ☎*624/143–8150*) has slightly smaller, less-luxurious boats that draw a young, party-oriented crowd. Four-hour trips cost $35 and include drinks, a light lunch, and equipment.

Buccaneer Queen (⊠*Solmar Hotel Cabo San Lucas* ☎*624/144-4217*) is a tall ship used in TV commercials that now carries passengers on snorkeling and sunset cruises.

SURFING

You can rent a board right at the beach in Todos Santos (see ⇨ Sidetrips).

SAN JOSÉ DEL CABO

Baja Salvaje (⊠*Obregón at Guerrero, San José del Cabo* ☎ *624/142–5300* ⊕*www.bajawild.com*) has daylong trips to surfing hot spots for beginners and experts. A fee of $85 per person includes transportation, equipment, and instruction at Costa Azul. Surf tours on the Pacific cost $105 per person.

THE CORRIDOR

For good surfing tips, rentals, and lessons, head to
Costa Azul Surf Shop (✉*Hwy. 1, Km 27.5, the Corridor*
☎*624/142–2771* ⊕*www.costa-azul.com.mx*). Surfboard
rentals are $20 a day and lessons are $55 all day, which
includes the surfboard.

Activities & Sports

WORD OF MOUTH

"Golf is a big draw in the area... [One&Only] Palmilla [and] Cabo del Sol are all great courses (so says my husband; I scuba dive). Reserve golf in advance (your concierge can help you). Whale-watching is [also] a big deal in Cabo; we actually could see them from our hotel. There are many companies that run whale-watching excursions; again your hotel should be able to provide a good suggestion."

—ellene

7

Revised
by Dan
Millington

IN THIS OCEAN-SIDE PLAYGROUND, where sport-fishing reigns supreme, the sea has long been the center for most activities. But Cabo's terrain lends itself to many sports and activities on land as well. Cactus fields, sand dunes, waterfalls, and mountain forests can be explored on foot, horseback, and on ATVs (all-terrain vehicles). Several tall rock faces make the area ideal for climbing and rappelling. Back in town, you can play beach volleyball on Playa Médano, tennis at most hotels or at the Fonatur complex, and get in a workout at your hotel or one of several gyms. For a less physically demanding outdoor activity, you can take a whale-watching or sunset cruise on one of the many tour boats.

Golf has lately become one of the biggest draws in Los Cabos. Much of the area's resources are being invested in the development of championship golf courses that serve as the centerpieces for enormous tourism developments.

SAN JOSÉ DEL CABO

BACKCOUNTRY TOURS

★ The folks at **Baja Wild** (⊠*Carretera 1, Km 31* ☎*624/142–5300* ⊕*www.bajawild.com*) always come up with adventures that are exciting. Hikes to canyons, hot springs, fossil beds, and caves with rock paintings expose you to the natural side of Cabo. Backcountry Jeep tours run from $95 to $125. Full-day kayak tours at Cabo Pulmo run $95 to $125. ATV tours in the desert with rappelling cost $85. Diving and rock climbing round out the options.

★ Longing to drive a Hummer? Go for it with **Baja Outback** (☎*624/172–6300* ⊕*www.bajaoutback.com*). They offer several day tours to the backcountry where you get to slide behind the wheel and terrify your friends as you dodge gullies and rocks. One option takes you to a remote mountain ranch before lunching and snorkeling at Cabo Pulmo. Day trips range from $165 to $220 per person. They also offer multiday tours exploring cave paintings and whale-watching at Magdalena Bay.

ECOTOURS

Trips with **Baja Salvaje** (⊠*Obregón at Guerrero, San José del Cabo* ☎*624/142–5300* ⊕*www.bajawild.com*) might include hikes to canyons, small waterfalls, hot springs, a fossil-rich area, or caves with rock paintings. You can also take a customized trip to La Sierra la Laguna, a series of mountain peaks submerged in water millions of years ago. The highest peak, at 7,000 feet above sea level, is ringed by pure pine forests. Rock-climbing and rappelling trips are also available. A seven-hour day trip includes breakfast, lunch, and hotel pickup and drop-off.

GOLF

Although most of the area's best golf courses are in the Corridor, Los Cabos's original course, **Campo del Golf San José** (⊠*Hwy. 1, Km 31.5, San José del Cabo* ☎*624/142–0905*), has wide fairways and few obstacles or slopes. It's good for beginners or as a warm-up. The well-maintained 18 holes are lined with residential properties (broken windows are not unusual). Some holes have nice ocean views, and there's a large lake near the bottom. It costs $99 to play 18 holes; twilight rate is $69 including cart rental.

ROCK CLIMBING

Three-hour trips with **Baja Salvaje** (⊠*Obregón at Guerrero, San José del Cabo* ☎*624/142–5300* ⊕*www.bajawild.com*) follow one of six routes. Four focus on rock climbing and two are dedicated to rappelling. Rock faces range from 120 feet to 320 feet, and some have extraordinary views of the ocean. Trips are designed for beginners or experts and can include as few as two people.

THE CORRIDOR

ATV TOURS

Desert Park (⊠*Cabo Real, across from Meliá Cabo Real, the Corridor* ☎*624/144-0127* ⊕*www.desertpark.net/html/index.html*) leads ATV tours seven times a day from 9 to 5 through the desert arroyos and canyons. The tours are more ecologically oriented than most, and guides point out geological formations and desert plants. Prices start at $50 per person.

BIKING

Bicycling isn't a major activity in Los Cabos. The lack of bike paths and the dangerous road conditions make it difficult to use bikes as a mode of transportation, and the heat quickly saps your energy. Mountain bikes are available for rent from **Desert Park** (⊠*Cabo Real, across from Meliá Cabo Real, the Corridor* ☎624/144–0127). Their mountain bike trails are far from public roads. Bikes rent for $15 an hour and $50 a day.

GOLF

Los Cabos has become one of the world's top golf destinations, thanks to Fonatur, Mexico's government tourism development agency, which decided to expand Los Cabos's appeal beyond sport-fishing. In 1988, the agency opened a nine-hole course in San José. Green fairways now appear like oases in the middle of the desert, with breathtaking holes alongside the Sea of Cortez.

Some courses in Cabo offer memberships, but most allow nonmembers to play. The exceptions are Querencia, designed by Tom Fazzio, and the El Dorado, designed by Jack Nicklaus. These courses, while said to be spectacular, are only open to members and their guests.

About a million gallons of water a day are required to maintain each course, which partially explains why courses charge some of the highest greens fees in the world. The cost usually includes access to the driving range, a golf cart, and bottled water. Some courses offer reduced rates for twilight play (after 3 PM). Greens fees are exorbitant—up to $350 in winter and $220 in summer. Rates given here are for high season, approximately November to May. Most hotels near the courses offer packages and reduced fees. Reservations are essential at all courses unless it's noted otherwise.

On the inland side of the Corridor, **Cabo del Sol Desert Course** (⊠*Hwy. 1, Km 10.3, the Corridor* ☎624/145–8200, 800/386–2405 in U.S. ⊕*www.cabodelsol.com*) is said to be "user-friendly": the longest hole is 625 yards, par 5. The course was designed by Tom Weiskopf. Special rates are available if you play both this and the Cabo del Sol Ocean Course. Greens fees start at $148 for twilight times, and $217 during the day.

Cabo del Sol Ocean Course (✉*Hwy. 1, Km 10.3, the Corridor* ☎*624/145–8200, 800/386–2405 in U.S.* ⊕*www. cabodelsol.com*) has been included in *Golf Digest*'s "Top 100 Courses in the World." According to designer Jack Nicklaus, it has the best three finishing holes in the world. On the par-3 17th hole, you drive over an ocean inlet with waves crashing below. The 18th hole is a mirror image of the 18th at Pebble Beach, California. Six holes are seaside. Greens fees start at $170 for twilight times, and $250 during the day.

The challenging **Cabo Real Golf Course** (✉*Hwy. 1, Km 19.5, the Corridor* ☎*624/144–0040, 877/795–8727 in U.S.* ⊕*www.caboreal.com*), designed by Robert Trent Jones II, has straight and narrow fairways, difficult slopes, and strategically placed bunkers. The first six holes are in mountainous terrain, working their way up to 500 feet above sea level. Recovering from mistakes here can be quite difficult. Three holes are oceanfront. The course played host to the PGA Senior Slam in 1996 and 1999. Greens fees for 18 holes are $280, and $154 at twilight.

The 27-hole **One&Only Palmilla Golf Course** (✉*Hwy. 1, Km 7.5, the Corridor* ☎*624/146–7000, 954/809–2726 in U.S.*) has wide fairways, gentle slopes, and large, challenging greens. On the 10th hole, you drive from a cliff, with the sea at your back; on the famous par-4 14th, you drive onto an island fairway. One hole borders the Sea of Cortez, and 12 holes have excellent sea views. It costs $210 and after 1 PM it's $135 for Palmilla guests and $255 with a twilight rate of $160 after 1 PM for nonguests to play nine holes. You can make reservations up to 60 days in advance.

HORSEBACK RIDING

☾ ★ The **Cuadra San Francisco Equestrian Center** (✉*Hwy. 1, Km 19.5, across from Cabo Real development, the Corridor* ☎*624/144–0160* ⊕*www.loscaboshorses.com*) gives trail rides and lessons. Its 45 beautiful show horses are well-trained. Trail rides go into the hills overlooking Cabo Real or to the San Carlos arroyo; both focus on the flora as much as the riding. Trips are limited to 20 people, with one guide for every six or seven people. Reserve at least a day in advance and request an English-speaking guide.

CABO SAN LUCAS

AIR TOURS

One of the most spectacular ways to view Baja is from the air. **Aéreo Calafia** (✉*Blvd. Marina at Plaza las Glorias, Cabo San Lucas* ☎*624/143–4302* ⊕*www.aereocalafia. com*) offers flights in small planes to Magdalena Bay where gray whales calve during winter months. The tours include the flight, a boat tour among the whales, and lunch, for $421 per person. Aéreo Calafia also offers air charters and specialized tours.

ATV TOURS

This is one of the most thrilling yet dangerous activities in Los Cabos. According to the local ambulance company, two or three people are injured every day (mostly sprains and broken bones). Accidents usually occur when operators take out huge groups with too few guides, lead them through major thoroughfares, and offer little or no instruction or safety tips. Know your trip's itinerary ahead of time. None of the companies have insurance, and they make you sign away your rights before going. But they do issue helmets, goggles, and handkerchiefs to protect you from the sand and dust.

When ATV trips are properly conducted, they can be safe and fun. The most popular trip passes through desert cactus fields, arrives at a big play area of large sand dunes with open expanses and specially carved trails, and ends at the old lighthouse. You can reach frighteningly high speeds as you descend the tall dunes. Navigating the narrow trails in the cactus fields is exciting but not for the weak-hearted or steering-impaired; you need to make sharp turns to avoid scraping into cactus, getting stuck in the sand, or toppling over. Another favorite trek travels past interesting rock formations, little creeks, and the beach on its way to a small mountain village called La Candelaria.

A three-hour trip costs about $60 for a single or $80 for a double (two people sharing an ATV). Six-hour trips to La Candelaria include lunch and cost about $110 for a single and $130 for a double. Wear tennis shoes, clothes you don't mind getting dirty, and a long-sleeve shirt or sweatshirt for afternoon tours in winter.

Tours are almost always full at **Baja's ATVs** (✉*Blvd. Marina, behind Tesoro Resort Hotel, Cabo San Lucas* ☎*624/143–2050*), so reserve a day in advance. Try the 9 AM or 12:30 PM departure for the lighthouse tour; the 4 PM tour is the most crowded and it returns at dark along some main roads. (ATVs kick up a lot of dust, reducing night visibility considerably.) A Candelaria trip leaves at 9 AM daily.

Cabo's Moto Rent (✉*Av. Cárdenas, in front of Puerto Paraíso, Cabo San Lucas* ☎*624/143–0808*) has a desert tour and a beach tour at Playa Migriño on the Pacific, along with the lighthouse and Candelaria tours. ATV rentals are available. **Tio Sports** (✉*Playa Médano, Cabo San Lucas* ☎*624/143–3399*) has lighthouse and Candelaria tours.

BOAT TOURS

The themes of Los Cabos boat tours vary, but all tours follow essentially the same route: through Bahía Cabo San Lucas, past El Arco and the sea-lion colony, around Land's End into the Pacific Ocean, and then east through the Sea of Cortez along the Corridor. Costs run about $40–$50 per person; all tours include an open bar.

Winter season whale-watching in the Sea of Cortez with **Cabo Expeditions** (✉*Tesoro Resort Hotel, Cabo San Lucas* ☎*624/143–2700*) is done from small, customized, inflatable Zodiac boats that allow passengers to get close to great gray and humpback whales. At times the whales even approach the boats with their babies. Fourteen passengers are allowed per tour.

The 60-foot sailboat ***Encore*** (✉*Cabo Isla Marina near Plaza Bonita, Cabo San Lucas* ☎*624/145–8383*) carries 30 passengers maximum. Whale-watching tours are offered in the morning from January to March, and sunset cruises are offered throughout the year. *Encore* tours are more sedate than those on the party boats.

The **Jungle Cruise** (✉*Tesoro Resort dock, Cabo San Lucas* ☎*624/143–7530*) is a typical booze cruise, with loud reggae and other party music. It attracts a twenty- to thirty-something crowd. It heads out from 10:30 AM to 2:30 PM and from 6 PM to 8 PM.

☼ *Kaleidoscope* (✉*marina near the Marina Fiesta hotel, Cabo San Lucas* ☎624/148–7318) is a luxurious, 100-foot power catamaran with comfortable seating inside and out. The whale-watching tour (10 AM to 12:30 PM) and the sunset cruise (5 to 7) are geared toward couples and families.

The double-decker party boat **Oceanus** (✉*Blvd. Marina, below El Galeón restaurant, Cabo San Lucas* ☎624/143–1059 ⊕*www.oceanusloscabos.com.mx*) has a sunset cruise with a live band. It leaves at 5 PM (6 PM in summer) from the main dock in Cabo San Lucas. You can rent the *Oceanus* for birthdays, weddings, and other special occasions.

Pez Gato (✉*Tesoro Resort dock, Cabo San Lucas* ☎624/143–3797 ⊕*www.pezgatocabo.com*) has two 42-foot catamarans, *Pez Gato I* and *Pez Gato II*. You can choose the tranquil, romantic sunset cruise or the rowdier "booze cruise." Sunset cruises depart from 5 to 7; there's no romantic sailing on Tuesday. A whale-watching cruise sails daily from 10:30 AM to 1:30 PM in winter.

☼ Cruises on the remarkable **Pirate Ship** (✉*Tesoro Resort dock, Cabo San Lucas* ☎624/143–4050 ⊕*www.pirateship-cabo.com*) built in 1885, are ideal for families with children. Deckhands dressed in pirate garb let kids help hoist the sail and tie knots, while they learn about the rich history of pirates in Cabo San Lucas. There's even a working cannon on board. The whale-watching trip uses hydrophones to listen to the whales' song. The 105-foot ship can hold 150 people. It sails from 10:30 to 1 and includes hot dogs and hamburgers. The two-hour sunset cruise departs at 5 from Monday through Saturday. Kids under age 12 ride free.

ECOTOURS

☼ **Eco Tours de Baja** (✉*Zaragoza at 5 de Febrero, Cabo San*
★ *Lucas* ☎624/143–0775) organizes a tour that includes a bumpy, exciting ride in a four-wheel-drive vehicle to a region rich with fossils, some millions of years old—you may even see a fossilized whale skeleton. Guides are knowledgeable and speak English. The area is protected by INAH, Mexico's National Institute of Anthropology and History, and several sites are being explored by scientists. During the ride you pass small ranches and vast fields of cardon cacti. Bird-watching is excellent early in the morning. Other tours include visits to the woodworking and leather factories in Miraflores and to waterfalls and lakes in the mountains.

Eyes in the Sky

CLOSE UP

An extraordinary variety of winged creatures color the landscape and skies of Los Cabos. Four distinct habitats—desert, ocean, pine forest, and tropical forest—afford great diversity of birds for such a small region. Cabo's location at the tip of a peninsula also makes it quite popular with migrating birds, who either stop here to rest in late autumn before venturing farther south or remain here through the winter.

Ten species of hummingbirds—including xanthus—along with the yellow-billed thrasher and

yellow-footed gull are some of the more watched-for species native to the area. Other species of particular interest to bird-watchers are cactus wrens, caracara, roadrunners, brown and white pelicans, the gila woodpecker, blue-footed boobies, and the endangered peregrine falcon. The best viewing spots can be found in the Sierra de la Laguna range and the freshwater estuaries in San José and Playa Las Palmas. The best times to spot birds are just after dawn and just before sunset.

Trips, which cost about $85, include a barbecue lunch at a small ranch, as well as hotel pickup and drop-off.

GOLF

Most of the courses in Los Cabos are attached to the large resorts in The Corridor. The lone course in Cabo San Lucias is renowned for spectacular views of the Sea of Cortez and El Arco—especially from the 18th hole—**Raven Golf Club** (⊠*Hwy. 1, Km 3.6, Cabo San Lucas* ☎624/143–4654 ☎888/328–8501 in U.S. ⊕*www.intrawestgolf.com*) has seven man-made lakes. The course was designed by the Dye Corporation. The signature hole is the par-5 7th. Eighteen holes are $180, with a twilight rate of $105.

GYMS

If your hotel or resort doesn't have a gym, a few in Cabo San Lucas allow short-term memberships. Fees average about $8 a day, $25 a week, and $45 a month.

Club Fit (⊠*Plaza Nautica, Blvd. Marina, Cabo San Lucas* ☎*No phone*) has excellent facilities, including a pool, free weights, and a variety of exercise machines. The club also

has aerobics and yoga classes and a health bar. Hours are
weekdays 6 AM–9:30 PM, Saturday 8–8, and Sunday 10–5.
The locals work out at **Gimnasio Rudos** (⊠*Av. Cárdenas and
Guerrero, Cabo San Lucas* ☎*624/143–0077*), a basic gym
with free weights and machines. There are showers for men
but not for women. It's open weekdays 6 AM–10 PM, Saturday 6 AM–8 PM.

HORSEBACK RIDING

Cantering down an isolated beach or up a desert trail is one
of the great pleasures of Los Cabos (as long as the sun isn't
beating down too heavily). The following companies have
well-fed and well-trained horses. One-hour trips generally
cost about $35 per person, two-hour trips about $65.

Horses are available for rent in front of the Playa Médano
hotels; contact **Rancho Collins Horses** (☎*624/143–3652*).

The popular **Red Rose Riding Stables** (⊠*Hwy. 1, Km 4, Cabo
San Lucas* ☎*624/143–4826*) has healthy horses for all levels of riders. The outfitter leads trips to the beach and the
desert. Groups are sometimes too large to suit all riders'
levels of expertise.

MOTORCYCLING

Hop on a Hog and live your own *Easy Rider* fantasy. The
Harley-Davidson Los Cabos in the Puerto Paraiso Entertain-
ment Plaza rents Electric Glides, Road Kings, and Heritage
Classics. Our suggested tour: ride northwest along the Old
East Cape Road in San José del Cabo until you reach Cabo
Pulmo. Rentals are $200 a day; additional days are $175.
☎*624/143–3337* ✐cabos@harley-davidson.com.mx.

WHALE-WATCHING

The gray-whale migration doesn't end at Baja's Pacific
lagoons. Plenty of whales of all sizes make it down to the
warmer waters off Los Cabos and into the Mar de Cortés.
To watch whales from shore, go to the beach at the Solmar
Suites, the Finesterra, or any Corridor hotel, or the lookout
points along the Corridor highway. Several companies run
trips (about $30–$50 depending on size of boat and length
of tour) from Cabo San Lucas. **Cabo Expeditions** (⊠*El Tesoro hotel, Blvd. Marina* ☎*624/143–2700*) offers snorkeling and whale-watching tours in rubber boats.

Shopping

8

Updated
by Dan
Millington

LOS CABOS MANUFACTURES SUNSHINE and a good time but very few products. One exception is glassware from La Fábrica de Vidrio Soplado (Blown-Glass Factory). In addition, a burgeoning arts scene has national and international artists opening galleries. Several shops will custom-design gold and silver jewelry for you, fashioning pieces in one to two days. Liquor shops sell a locally produced liqueur called damiana, touted as an aphrodisiac.

Despite Cabo's lack of homegrown wares, stores are filled with beautiful and unusual items from mainland Mexico. You can find hand-painted blue Talavera tiles from Puebla; blue-and-yellow pottery from Guanajuato; black pottery from the village of San Bartolo Coyotepec (near Oaxaca); hammocks from the Yucatán; embroidered clothing from Oaxaca, Chiapas, and the Yucatán; silver jewelry from Taxco; opals from Queretaro; and the fine beaded crafts of the Huichol tribe from Nayarit and Jalisco.

ABOUT THE STORES

Many stores, especially those that fan out from the central plaza in San José del Cabo and from the marina in San Lucas, open daily around 10 AM and close by 9 PM. Some shops still close at noon or 1 for a one- to two-hour lunch break. If cruise ships are in port, shops open early and stay open as long as the day-trippers are around.

Credit cards are widely accepted, though many places do not accept American Express. Most stores readily accept U.S. dollars but usually give change in pesos. Sticker prices appear in pesos or dollars—sometimes it's difficult to tell. Ask before you get too carried away, and carry a calculator for quick conversions.

Most enclosed shops do not bargain. Still, if you're buying a large quantity of items at one shop, you can always ask for a discount. Bargaining is acceptable when you go to a *tianguis* (arts-and-crafts market) and at the sidewalk market along the marina, but it may not be worth the effort.

Not all salespeople are fluent in English, especially in crafts shops, so use whatever Spanish you know and speak slowly.

Bead by Bead

To place and glue the tiny beads that will turn a carved wooden jaguar the size of a small cat into a colorful work of art, it takes a Huichol Indian a full day—not to mention a steady hand. A small carving of a deer, considered a messenger of the gods to guide the shamans (priests who use magic to treat ailments) during ceremonies, may take only an hour. These unusual pieces can be found at the **Huichol Collection** in Cabo San Lucas. The sale of authentic ceremo-nial works of art, artifacts, and handicrafts helps to support the Huichol people. (The deer figurine, for instance, goes for about 200 pesos, or about $21.) Until recently, the Huichol, a tribe of shamans and artists, lived undisturbed in the rugged Sierra Madre in Nayarit and Jalisco. They are one of the few indigenous groups in the world to have retained their original culture. Approximately 8,000 still survive, keeping alive a spiritual, nature-based way of life.

NEIGHBORHOODS & MALLS

Near where the fishing boats come in at the Cabo San Lucas marina, the **Mercado de Artesanías** (Crafts Market ⊠ *South end of Blvd. Marina, Cabo San Lucas*) sells pottery, blankets, jewelry, and Mexican sombreros.

The palatial entrance to **Puerto Paraíso** (⊠*Av. Cárdenas, Cabo San Lucas*) leads into a three-story marble- and glass-enclosed mall. Though at this writing, the mall is not yet full, it's quickly becoming a social center of San Lucas. Kaki Bassi, a well-known local artist, has opened a gallery, as has Sergio Bustamante. Clothing shops include Cotton Club, Guess, and quicksilver, plus several beachwear boutiques. If you're hungry, check out the two Häagen-Dazs shops, Johnny Rockets diner, or Ruth's Chris Steak House. A bowling alley and a complex of movie theaters take care of your entertainment needs.

Plaza Aramburo (⊠*Av. Cárdenas and Av. Zaragoza, Cabo San Lucas*) is a primarily service-oriented shopping area with a pharmacy, bank, dry cleaner, and grocery store. But it also has clothing and swimwear shops.

A pleasant place to stroll, **Plaza Bonita** (⊠*Blvd. Marina at Av. Cárdenas, Cabo San Lucas*) has restaurants, bars, and a few shops.

People in Glass Houses

A beautiful glass mosaic over the entrance to La Fábrica de Vidrio Soplado (Blown-Glass Factory) welcomes Los Cabos's most famous artisans every day. Founded in 1988 by engineer Sebastian Romo, the factory uses a glassmaking process close to the one first developed in western Asia 4,000 years ago, later refined into glassblowing during the Roman empire.

At the factory, 35 artisans produce more than 450 pieces a day from hundreds of pounds of locally recycled glass. Tourists watch while crushed recycled glass is liquefied in gas-fired ovens and, seconds later, transformed into exquisite figures. Secrets for making the thick glassware's deep blues, greens, and reds—the result of special mixtures of metals and gold—are passed from generation to generation.

You are sometimes invited to make your own glassware by blowing through a hollow rod to shape a glob of molten glass at the end. The results are usually not impressive. The factory is in the industrial area of Cabo San Lucas and is usually open to the public Monday through Saturday 8 to 2.

Plaza del Mar (⊠*Av. Cárdenas, Cabo San Lucas*), across from the Plaza Bonita mall, sells T-shirts, tank tops, sweat-shirts, and more at its souvenir boutiques.

Bordering the Cabo San Lucas marina is the **Plaza Nautica** (⊠*Blvd. Marina, Cabo San Lucas*), where you can find resort wear, jewelry, furniture, fine art, and a number of eateries.

SPECIALTY SHOPS

SAN JOSÉ DEL CABO

San José has the best shopping for high-quality folk art, jewelry, and home furnishings. Some of the finest shops are clustered around Plaza Mijares where Boulevard Mijares and Avenida Zaragoza both end at a pedestrian walkway. For fresh produce, flowers, meat, fish, and a sampling of local life in San José, visit the **Mercado Municipal,** off Calle Doblado.

ART GALLERIES

The art scene is steadily improving, and art walks are held by the galleries every Thursday night.

The architecture at **Galería de ida Victoria** (⊠*Calle Guerrero 1128* ☎*624/142–5772*) is nearly as fascinating as the international art. The two-story building was designed as a gallery, with skylights and domes for natural light. Several other interesting galleries are nearby.

Pez Gordo (⊠*Obregón 19* ☎*624/142–5788*) displays original works by local artists.

★ **Veryka** (⊠*Blvd. Mijares 6B* ☎*624/142–0575*) is associated with galleries in San Miguel de Allende and Oaxaca, two of Mexico's finest art centers. The *huipiles* (embroidered blouses), masks, tapestries, and pottery here are coveted by collectors. Prices are high, but so is the quality.

BOOKS

The bookstore **Libros** (⊠*Blvd. Mijares 41* ☎*624/142–4433*) stocks a good selection of magazines, as well as the *Wall Street Journal* and *USA Today.*

CLOTHING FOR CHILDREN

Curios Alberto (⊠*Av. Zaragoza in front of Plaza Mijares* ☎*No phone*) carries beautiful embroidered dresses for young girls.

FOLK ART

Several gems are clustered along the side streets off Mijares. **ADD** (⊠*Av. Zaragoza at Calle Hidalgo* ☎*624/143–2055*) is an interior-design shop that has hand-painted dishes from Guanajuato, carved wood furniture from Michoacán, and unique Christmas decorations.

El Armario (⊠*Calle Obregon at Calle Morelos* ☎*No phone*) displays modern folk art, frames made from cactus wood, posters, and a clever assortment of souvenirs.

Copal (⊠*Plaza Mijares* ☎*624/142–3070*) has carved animals from Oaxaca, masks from Guerrero Negro, and heavy wooden furnishings.

The array of Mexican textiles, pottery, glassware, hammocks, and souvenirs at **Curios Carmela** (⊠*Blvd. Mijares 43* ☎*624/142–1117*) is overwhelming, and the prices are reasonable. You could easily find all the gifts you need right here.

★ **Galería Veryka** (✉*Blvd. Mijares 6-B* ☎*624/142–0575*) is the best folk art shop in the region, with gorgeous embroidered clothing, masks, wood carvings, jewelry, and hand-molded black and green pottery. Nearly everything is from Oaxaca. Check out the seasonal displays, especially the Day of the Dead altar.

An offshoot of a longstanding San Lucas shop, **Necri** (✉*Blvd. Mijares 16* ☎*624/130–7500*) carries ceramics, pottery, and pewter pieces and hot sauce made by the owner.

JEWELRY

Amethyst (✉*Blvd. Mijares and Doblado* ☎*624/142–4160*) carries rings, bracelets, and necklaces with precious and semiprecious stones, including Mexican opal. Custom designs can be made in a few hours; complex designs may take a couple of days.

Sax (✉*Blvd. Mijares 2* ☎*624/142–0704*) displays handcrafted silver jewelry. The artists will create a design of your choice in 24 hours.

SUNDRIES & LIQUOR

If your needs are more practical, stop into **Almacenes Goncanseco** (✉*Blvd. Mijares 18, across from El Palacio Municipal* ☎*No phone*), which sells film, postcards, groceries, and liquor.

Los Barriles de Cuervo (✉*Blvd. Mijares at Juárez* ☎*624/142–5322*) specializes in rare tequilas.

Away from the tourist zone is San José's traditional market area, **El Mercado San José** (✉*Castro at Coronado* ☎*No phone*), where you can stock your kitchen(ette) with fresh meats and produce, or visit the market's **Viva Mexico** stand for clothes, belts, spices, jewelry, and other random items—all at excellent prices.

TOBACCO

Los Amigos Smokeshop and Cigar Bar (✉*Calle Doblado and Morelos* ☎*624/142–1138*) is a classy shop and cigar bar with fine Cuban and Mexican cigars and Casa Noble tequila. Look for visiting celebrities here.

THE CORRIDOR

Along the Corridor, shopping is limited to hotel gift shops, a couple of artisans' markets that cater to busloads of cruise-ship passengers, a few strip malls, and a much-celebrated Costco warehouse store.

La Europa (⊠*Hwy. 1, Km 6.7* ☎*624/145–8755*) carries a wide selection of imported wines and deli products.

Trader Dicks (⊠*Hwy. 1, Km 29.5* ☎*624/142–2828*) is a favorite with Americans seeking newspapers from home, along with familiar deli meats and cheeses.

CABO SAN LUCAS

Boulevard Marina and the side streets between the waterfront and the main plaza are filled with small shops. At the crafts market in the marina you can pose for a photo with an iguana, plan a ride in a glass-bottom boat, or browse through stalls packed with blankets, sombreros, and pottery.

ART GALLERIES

★ The second-floor **Golden Cactus Gallery** (⊠*Guerrero and Madero* ☎*624/143–6399*), run by artists Chris MacClure and Marilyn Hurst, has been showcasing local artists' work since 1997. Bill Clinton is among those with MacClure's pieces in their collections.

★ The **Kaki Bassi Gallery** (⊠*Morelos and Alikan* ☎*624/143–3510* ⊠*Puerto Paraíso, Av. Cárdenas* ☎*624/144–4510*) displays works by Kaki Bassi, who has exhibited all over Europe and has seven pieces of art in the Mexican government's permanent collection. Her gallery exhibits many Mexican artists.

BOOKS

Libros (⊠*Blvd. Marina at Plaza de la Danza* ☎*624/143–3173*) carries a vast number of Spanish- and English-language novels and magazines.

CAMERAS & FILM

Foto Fuji (⊠*Morelos at Blvd. Marina* ☎*624/143–2020*) has one-hour film developing and sells film, batteries, videotapes, and cameras.

CLOTHING

Cotton Club (✉*Puerto Paraíso, Av. Cárdenas* ☎*624/143–2388*) stocks women's resort wear—of natural fibers only—by Mexican and international designers.

Dos Lunas (✉*Plaza Bonita, Blvd. Marina* ☎*624/143–1969* ✉*Puerto Paraíso, Blvd. Marina* ☎*624/143–1969*) is full of trendy, colorful sportswear and straw hats.

Need a new bathing suit? Swimwear at **H2O de los Cabos** (✉*Madero at Guerrero* ☎*624/143–1219*) ranges from skimpy thongs to modest one-piece suits.

★ A favorite of locals and Cabo regulars, **Magic of the Moon** (✉*Hidalgo off Blvd. Marina* ☎*624/143–3161*) has unique clothing designed by Pepita, the owner. If you don't see what you want, she can design an outfit for you and have it made in three days. Check out her handmade ceramic jewelry and beaded bustiers.

Tropica Calipso (✉*Puerto Paraíso, Blvd. Marina* ☎*624/143–9792*) sells resort wear; both men and women can have an outfit custom-made in 24 hours.

COFFEE

★ The aroma of roasting coffee beans lures caffeine junkies to the **Cabo Coffee Company** (✉*Madero at Hidalgo* ☎*624/105–1130*). Organic green coffee beans are flown fresh from Oaxaca to the Los Cabos shop, where they are roasted and bagged for sale. The store sells flavored coffee, chai tea, and ice cream as well.

FOLK ART

One of the oldest folk art shops in the area, **Faces of Mexico** (✉*Av. Cárdenas, beside Mar de Cortés hotel* ☎*624/143–2634*) has a selection of masks from Oaxaca and Guerrero, though the owner's collection of handmade masks at the back of the tiny shop is far more interesting than the manufactured versions for sale up front.

The **Huichol Collection** (✉*Blvd. Marina and Ocampo* ☎*624/143–4055*) carries the Huichol Indian tribe's beautiful beaded crafts, as well as posters, postcards, and T-shirts in the vibrant colors and patterns typical of this ancient culture.

Necri (✉*Blvd. Marina between Madero and Ocampo* ☎*624/143–0283*) has an excellent selection of folk art and home furnishings.

FOOD

Locals appreciate the selection of imported wines, cheeses, pâtés, and other gourmet delicacies, including organic foods, at **Tutto Bene** (⊠*Blvd. Marina near Calle San Lucas* ☎*624/144–3300*).

GIFTS

Mama Eli's (⊠*Av. San Lucas* ☎*624/143–1616*) is a three-story gallery with fine furnishings, ceramics, appliquéd clothing, and children's toys.

The funky Cabo Wabo bar sells souvenirs in its **Waboutique** (⊠*Guerrero* ☎*624/143–1188*).

GLASS

Handblown glass pieces in vivid colors are sold at **La Fábrica de Vidrio Soplado** (*Blown-Glass Factory*) (⊠*2 blocks west of Hwy. 1* ☎*624/143–0255*) on the outskirts of Cabo San Lucas, near the bypass road to Todos Santos. Drive toward San José on Avenida Cárdenas, which turns into Highway 1. The factory is in an industrial area two blocks northwest of Highway 1, off the bypass to Todos Santos.

HOME FURNISHINGS

★ Homeowners and restaurateurs from throughout the area shop for furnishings, dishes, and glassware at **Artesanos** (⊠*Carretera 1, Km 4* ☎*624/143–3850*).

Cartes (⊠*Plaza Bonita, Blvd. Marina* ☎*624/143–1770*) has hand-painted pottery and tableware, pewter frames, hand-blown glass, and carved furniture.

★ **El Callejón** (⊠*Guerrero between Av. Cárdenas and Madero* ☎*624/143–1139*) is known for gorgeous furniture, lamps, dishes, and pottery.

Walk around the marina from Plaza Bonita to **Galería Gate-melatta** (⊠*Calle Gómez Farias, road to Hotel Hacienda* ☎*624/143–1166*), where the specialties are colonial furniture and antiques.

JEWELRY

★ Gorgeous silver jewelry created by the Brilanti family of Taxco is on display at **Joyería Brilanti** (⊠*Guerrero between Madero and Zapata* ☎*624/105–1664* ⊕*www.brilanti. com*). The family's work has been included in museum shows in the United States and is coveted by collectors.

LEATHER GOODS

Gold Duck (✉*Plaza Nautica, Blvd. Marina* ☎624/143–2335) sells leather products, including handbags, belts, and wallets.

LINENS

Choose from the many serapes and cotton blankets at **Cuca's Blanket Factory** (✉*Av. Cárdenas at Matamoros* ☎624/143–1913). You can design your own and have it ready the next day.

TOBACCO & LIQUOR

Cuban and international cigars are sold at **J&J Habanos** (✉*Madero and Blvd. Marina* ☎624/143–6160), as is tequila, Cuban coffee, and clothing.

Side Trips

WORD OF MOUTH

"I love La Paz so much that I moved here permanently in September from the USA. Do not come to La Paz if you want World Heritage Site architecture, great museums, or a hard-core clubbing scene. Do come to La Paz if you want to relax and meet real Mexicans in a laid-back atmosphere. Hit the beaches. They are wonderful. You can get to some by walking or by taking a bus, but I'd recommend renting a car for at least some of the time here. This will give you easy access to the best beaches."

—DRMIKEPHD

Updated
by Dan
Millington

A CHANGE OF SCENERY can be welcome after a few days of sun worshipping, beachcombing, and tequila tasting in Los Cabos. If you're venturing out just for the day, tranquil **Todos Santos, La Paz** (the capital of Baja Sur), and the **East Cape** are easy side trips. The first two carve different slices of Baja culture: one is a small village centered on the arts; the other is the region's bustling capital. If natural wonders are more to your taste, the East Cape, including the small communities of Buena Vista and Los Barriles, can satisfy with secluded coves and beautiful vistas.

Whether you rent a car or jeep, take a guided tour, or hop on the bus depends largely on where you want to go. The comfortable (air-conditioned and rest-room–equipped) bus makes your journey relatively carefree, but if you like to explore along the way, renting a car allows you more freedom. Do not drive on the highways after dark, as there are no fences to keep animals off the roads and dips in the roads sometimes flood.

If you'd like to spend some serious time away from the tourist mecca of Los Cabos, there are a number of places to stay the night in Todos Santos, La Paz, and the East Cape (⇨ *Where to Stay*), including the Hotel California, Todos Santos Inn, and Posada la Poza in Todos Santos; el ángel azul and La Concha Beach Resort in La Paz; and Hotel Buena Vista and Hotel Palmas de Cortez in the East Cape.

TODOS SANTOS

72 km (45 mi) north of Cabo San Lucas.

Artists from throughout the Southwest (and a few from Mexico) have found a haven in this small town near the Pacific coast north of Los Cabos. Architects and entrepreneurs have restored early-19th-century adobe and brick buildings around the main plaza, and speculators have laid out housing tracts in the rocky hills between the town and the shore, contributing to a rapid rise in real-estate prices. In high season, tour buses on day trips from Los Cabos often clog the streets around the plaza. When the buses leave, the town is a peaceful place to wander.

Los Cabos visitors and locals typically take day trips here, though there are several small inns that provide a peaceful antidote to Cabo's noise and crowds. El Pescadero, the largest settlement before Todos Santos, is home to ranchers and farmers who grow herbs and vegetables. Be sure to head back to Cabo from Todos Santos before dark, because Carretera 19 between the two towns is unlighted and prone to high winds and flooding. And don't be tempted to try the dirt roads that intersect the highway unless you're in a four-wheel-drive vehicle. Sands on the beach or in the desert stop conventional vehicles in their tracks.

Business hours are erratic, especially in September and October. Be sure to pick up *El Calendario de Todos Santos,* a free English-language guide with events and developments. It's available at many hotels, shops, and restaurants.

WHERE TO EAT

$$-$$$ ✕**Cafe Santa Fe.** The setting, with tables in an overgrown ★ courtyard, is as appealing as the food: salads and soups made from organic vegetables and herbs, homemade pastas, and fresh fish with light herbal sauces. Many Cabo residents lunch here weekly. The marinated seafood salad is a sublime blend of shrimp, octopus, and mussels with olive oil and garlic, with plenty for two to share before dining on lobster ravioli. ⊠*Calle Centenario* ☎*612/145–0340* ⊟*MC, V* ☉*Closed Tues. and parts of Sept. and Oct.*

$-$$ ✕**Los Adobes.** Locals swear by the fried, cilantro-studded local cheese and the beef tenderloin with *huitlacoche* (a savory mushroomlike fungus) at this pleasant outdoor restaurant. The menu is ambitious and includes tapas and several vegetarian options—rare in these parts. At night the place sparkles with star-shape lights. The Internet café within the restaurant has high-speed access. ⊠*Calle Hidalgo* ☎*612/145–0203* ⊟*MC, V* ☉*No dinner Sun.*

$-$$ ✕**Caffé Todos Santos.** Omelets, bagels, granola, and wholegrain breads delight the breakfast crowd at this small café; deli sandwiches, fresh salads, and an array of tamales, *flautas* (tortillas rolled around savory fillings), and combo plates are lunch and dinner highlights. Check for fresh seafood on the daily specials board. ⊠*Calle Centenario 33* ☎*612/145–0300* ⊟*No credit cards* ☉*No lunch and dinner Mon.*

$-$$ **Tequila's Sunrise.** Owner Manuel Valdez's damiana margaritas (made with fine tequila, fresh squeezed lime juice, and damiana, a sweet liqueur) and shrimp chiles rellenos have been a hit here since 1980. All ingredients are organic and

9

Driver's Beware

Despite a paucity of traffic lights, the small towns of Baja California Sur (outside Los Cabos) are small enough that vehicular traffic is typically not a problem. Indeed, during high season pedestrians are usually more bothersome than cars.

Indeed, the greatest road hazards are cows, sudden potholes, dips (*vados*), and roadwork, which make it dangerous to drive after dark. Even during daylight hours, narrow roads and open ranges that allow cattle to wander where they

please can be dangerous. En route to Todos Santos and La Paz, crosses and flowers at accident sites are grim reminders that fatalities on the road are all too frequent.

Stick to posted speed limits, usually 90 kph (55 mph) on the highways and 40 kpm (25 mph) in town (signs are always posted in kilometers and in Spanish). Pemex service stations are abundant, but it's a good idea to keep your gas tank at least half full.

locally grown—so go on, order the chocolate cake mixed with flan and topped with an Ameretto-Kahlua chocolate sauce. Be sure to add your John Hancock to the others on the walls before you go. ⊠*On Juárez Av., across from Hotel California* ☎*612/145–0073* ☰*MC, V.*

$-$$ ✕ **El Zaguán.** It's worth the wait for one of the marble-
★   topped tables at dinner at this teeny locals' joint—you'll see what we mean when you tuck into fresh seafood dishes prepared with sauces and herbs (fillet of dorado in basil butter is our favorite), or organic salads. *Palo de Arco* (woven, indigenous wood from the Baja) adorns the walls. If you have a larger group, you can find seating for six in the back. ⊠*Juárez Av. between Hidalgo and Topete Calles* ☎*612/145–0017* ☰*No credit cards* ⊙*Closed Sun.*

WHERE TO STAY

$$-$$$ ⌂ **Hotel California.** This handsome structure has undergone
★   extensive remodeling over several years and is now at its best ever, thanks to the artistic bent of owners John and Debbie Stewart. A deep blue and ocher color scheme runs throughout, and rooms, some with ocean views, have a mix of antiques and folk art. The Coronela restaurant and bar are local hot spots, and the Emporio shop is stuffed with curiosities. ⊠*Calle Juárez, at Morelos, 23305* ☎*612/145–*

0525 ⛵*11 rooms* ⚑*In-room: no a/c (some), no phone, no TV. In-hotel: restaurant, bar, pool, no elevator* ⊟*MC, V.*

$$–$$$ ✗**Posada La Poza.** The Swiss owners aim to please with their chic posada beside a bird-filled lagoon and the open sea. The handsome suites have rust-tone walls, modern furniture, and Swiss linens; a CD player and binoculars are on hand, but there aren't any TVs or phones. Even if you're not staying, stop by the restaurant ($$–$$$; closed Thurs.) for spicy tortilla soup, local scallops, and organic salads. ⊠*Follow signs on Carretera 19 and on Av. Juárez to beach, 23305* ☎*612/145–0400* ⊕*www.lapoza.com* ⛵*7 suites* ⚑*In-room: no phone, safe, no TV, refrigerator. In-hotel: restaurant, bar, pool, public Internet, no elevator* ⊟*MC, V* ⚑*BP.*

$$–$$$ ⛱**Todos Santos Inn.** The eight guest rooms in this converted 19th-century house are unparalleled in design and comfort. Gorgeous antiques are set against stone walls under brick ceilings. Ceiling fans and the shade from garden trees keep the rooms cool and breezy. The absence of telephones and TVs makes a perfect foil for the conceits of Los Cabos. The wine bar is open in the evening, and good restaurants are within easy walking distance. ⊠*Calle Legaspi, 23305* ☎☎*612/145–0040* ⊕*www.todossantosinn.com* ⛵*6 rooms* ⚑*In-room: no a/c (some), no phone, no TV. In-hotel: bar, no elevator* ⊟*MC, V.*

MUSICAL MYTH Ignore rumors that the Eagles song originated at this Hotel California. It didn't. Your call whether or not to buy the T-shirts and tequila emblazoned with the name that are on sale here.

9

SHOPPING

A leader on the art scene is the **Charles Stewart Gallery & Studio** (⊠*Calle Centenario at Calle Obregón* ☎*612/145–0265*). Stewart moved from Taos, New Mexico, to Todos Santos in 1986, and is credited as one of the founders of the town's artist community. Some of his paintings and art pieces have a Baja or Mexican theme. His studio is in one of the town's loveliest 19th-century buildings. **Fénix de Todos Santos** (⊠*Calle Juárez at Calle Topete* ☎*612/145–0666*) has bowls and plates from Tonalá, handblown glassware, Talavera pottery, and cotton clothing by the designer Sucesos.

At **Galería Santa Fé** (⊠ *Calle Centenario 4* ☎ *612/145–0340*), in an 1850s adobe building, Paula and Ezio Colombo sell collector-quality folk art including frames adorned with images of Frida Kahlo and her art, kid-size chairs decorated with bottle caps, Virgin of Guadalupe images, and *milagros* (small tin charms used as offerings to saints). **Galería de Todos Santos** (⊠ *Calle Topete and Calle Legaspi* ☎ *612/145–0040*), owned by Michael and Pat Cope, displays Michael's modern art and exhibits works by international artists living in Baja. The gallery is one of the focal points for the ever-changing local arts scene.

Filled with gorgeous Guatemalan textiles, Mexican folk art, belts, purses, wood carvings, and Day of the Dead figurines, **Mangos** (⊠ *Calle Centenario across from Charles Stewart Gallery* ☎ *612/145–0451*) is an intriguing shop. The best bookstore in the Los Cabos region is **El Tecolote Bookstore** (⊠ *Calle Juárez at Calle Hidalgo* ☎ *612/145–0295*). Stop here for Latin American literature, poetry, children's books, current fiction and nonfiction, and books on Baja.

SURFING

You can rent a board right on the beach at **Todos Santos Surf Shop** (⊠ *Playa Los Cerritos, Hwy. 19, Km 64, near Todos Santos* ☎ *044–612/108–0709 cell phone*).

TODOS SANTOS ESSENTIALS

Whether you're driving or taking the local bus, the best route to Todos Santos is Highway 19, traveling along the Pacific Ocean from Cabo San Lucas. Linking Todos Santos with the rest of the Baja Peninsula, the road narrows from four lanes to two at times, and goes up and down like a mild roller coaster. Once you reach Todos Santos, the town is compact enough for you to get around on foot.

BY BUS

Águila buses depart the **Cabo San Lucas bus station** (⊠ *Calle 5 de Febrero, at Carretera Todos Santos* ☎ *624/143–7878*) every hour. The trip takes about 90 minutes. In Todos Santos, the bus stops at open-air Pilar's Fresh Fish Tacos restaurant. Drivers don't make announcements. Return buses leave every hour from across the street; the last one usually departs at 7 PM, but be sure to ask, since the schedule changes. Bus fare is $5 each way, paid in pesos or U.S. dollars at the station in San Lucas and on the bus.

BY CAR

The trip to Todos Santos takes about an hour by car. A sign points the way to Highway 19 from Highway 1 north of San Lucas. The sign reads CARRETERA A TODOS SANTOS; follow this road to the first major intersection, and then turn right. Don't drive on the highway at night, and don't explore dirt roads off the highway unless you're in a four-wheel-drive vehicle; if you aren't, getting stuck in the sand is a strong possibility. Most streets in the center of Todos Santos have no-parking signs; look for space on side streets.

BY VAN TOUR

Full-day van tours from Los Cabos to Todos Santos cost about $65 per person including breakfast, snacks, and drinks. **Contactours** (⊠ *Av. Zaragoza at 5 de Febrero, San José del Cabo* ☎624/143–2439) will provide a van and guide for private tours. **Rancho Tours** (⊠ *Libertad, at 20 de Noviembre, Cabo San Lucas* ☎624/143–5464) also has full-day van tours. **Transcabo Tours** (⊠ *Hwy. 1, Km 43 San José del Cabo* ☎624/146–0888) offers tours to Todos Santos for $50; lunch is not included.

LA PAZ

195 km (121 mi) north of San José del Cabo.

La Paz may be the capital of Baja Sur and home to about 200,000 residents, but it feels like a small town in a time warp. It's the most traditional Mexican city in Baja Sur, the antithesis of the gringolandia developments to the south. Granted, there are plenty of foreigners in La Paz, particularly during snowbird season. But in the slowest part of the off-season, during the oppressive late-summer heat, you can easily see how La Paz aptly translates as "the peace," and its residents can be called *paceños* (peaceful ones). The city sprawls inland from the curve of its malécon along the Bahía La Paz, which, through some strange feat of geography, angles west toward the sunset.

Travelers use La Paz as both a destination in itself and a stopping-off point en route to Los Cabos. There's always excellent scuba diving and sportfishing in the Sea of Cortez. La Paz is the base for divers and fishermen headed for Cerralvo, La Partida, and the Espíritu Santo islands, where

CLOSE UP

Old Baja & New

The Baja of yesteryear had two faces. One was of the upscale resort where celebrities hid out, having flown down—usually from California—in private planes; the other was of a parade of "trailers," aluminum boxes barely big enough for two people. Free spirits drove these homes-on-wheels throughout Baja California, camping overnight in trailer parks along the way. They came to commune with like-minded souls, seek oneness with nature, and just "be" in the remote beauty of southern Baja.

Times have changed, with the Baja-bound landing somewhere between the extremes of yesteryear. Trailer parks still exist, but today's sophisticated offspring come complete with power hookups and enjoy the luxuries of restaurants and nightly entertainment. Those aluminum boxes have given way to modern recreational vehicles, some larger and more luxurious than two-bedroom apartments. And instead of celebrities descending in private planes, today people from all walks of life pour off some 30 commercial flights a day into the San José International Airport.

parrot fish, manta rays, neons, and angels blur the clear waters by the shore, and marlin, dorado, and yellowtail leap from the sea. Cruise ships are more and more often spotted sailing toward the bay as La Paz emerges as an attractive port.

La Paz officially became the capital of Baja California Sur in 1974, and is the state's largest settlement (though Los Cabos is quickly catching up. There are few chain hotels or restaurants now, but the region, including parts of the coastline south of the city, is slated to have several large-scale, high-end resort developments with golf courses, marinas, and vacation homes.

WHAT TO SEE

★ The **Malecón** is La Paz's seawall, tourist zone, and social center all rolled into one. It runs along Paseo Alvaro Obregón and has a sidewalk as well as several park areas in the sand just off it. Paceños are fond of strolling the malecón at sunset. Teenagers slowly cruise the street in their spiffed-up cars, couples nuzzle on park benches, and grandmothers slowly walk along while keeping an eye on the kids. The malecón is undergoing a face-lift: stonework and wrought iron street lamps line the walkway, and it's being extended all the way north to Playa Coromuel. Marina La Paz, at the malecón's southwest end, is an ever-growing development with condominiums, vacation homes, and a pleasant café-lined walkway.

A two-story white gazebo is the focus of **Malecón Plaza,** a small concrete square where musicians sometimes appear on weekend nights. Across the street, Calle 16 de Septiembre leads inland to the city.

Plaza Constitución, the true center of La Paz, is a traditional zócalo, which also goes by the name Jardín Velazco. Concerts are held in the park gazebo and locals gather here for art shows and fairs.

La Catedral de Nuestra Señora de la Paz, the downtown church, is a simple stone building with a modest gilded altar. The church was built in 1860 near the site of La Paz's first mission, which was established that same year by Jesuit Jaime Bravo. ⊠ *Calle Juárez* ☎ *No phone.*

La Paz's culture and heritage are well represented at the **Museo de Antropología,** which has re-creations of Comondu and Las Palmas Indian villages, photos of cave paintings found in Baja, and copies of Cortés's writings on first sighting La Paz. Many exhibit descriptions are written only in Spanish, but the museum's staff will help you translate. ⊠ *Calle Altamirano, at Calle 5 de Mayo, Centro* ☎ *612/122–0162* ☎ *Donation requested* ☉ *Daily 9–6.*

9

The former governor's mansion is gradually being transformed into an aquarium called **Museo Acuario de las Californias,** on the road to Pichilingue. Featuring the marine life in the Sea of Cortez, the tanks containing lobster, corals, and rays are inside the building, while the exterior has ponds and waterfalls. The house faces a coral reef; plans in the works include snorkeling programs and educational workshops. ⊠ *Carretera a Pichilingue, Km 7* ☎ *No phone* ☎ *Donation requested* ☉ *Daily 10–2.*

BEACHES

Along the malecón, stick to ambling along the sand while watching local families enjoy the sunset. Just north of town the beach experience is much better; it gets even better north of Pichilingue. Save your swimming and snorkeling energies for this area.

Playa Balandra. A rocky point shelters a clear, warm bay at Playa Balandra, 21 km (13 mi) north of La Paz. Several small coves and beaches appear and disappear with the tides, but there's always a calm area where you can wade and swim. Snorkeling is fair at the coral reef at Balandra's south end. You may spot clams, starfish, and anemones. Kayaking and snorkeling tours usually set into the water here. If not on a tour, bring your own gear, as rentals aren't normally available. The beach has a few palapas for shade, barbecue pits, and trash cans. Camping is permitted but there are no hookups. The beach gets crowded on weekends, but on a weekday morning you may have the place to yourself. There are plans for a resort development here, but construction has not begun.

Playa Caimancito. La Concha hotel takes up some of the sand at the beach 5 km (3 mi) north of La Paz. But you can enter the beach north and south of the hotel and enjoy a long stretch of sand facing the bay and downtown. Locals swim laps here, as the water is almost always calm and salty enough for easy buoyancy. There aren't any facilities, but if you wander over to the hotel for lunch or a drink you can use their restrooms and rent water toys.

Playa Pichilingue. Starting in the time of Spanish invaders, Pichilingue, 16 km (10 mi) north of La Paz, was known for its preponderance of oysters bearing black pearls. In 1940 a disease killed them off, leaving the beach deserted. Today it's a pleasant place to sunbathe and watch sportfishing boats bring in their hauls. Locals set up picnics here on weekend afternoons and linger until the blazing sun settles into the bay. Restaurants consisting of little more than a palapa over plastic tables and chairs serve oysters *diablo*, fresh clams, and plenty of cold beer. Pichilingue curves northeast along the bay to the terminals where the ferries from Mazatlán and Topolobampo arrive and many of the sportfishing boats depart. The water here, though not particularly clear, is calm enough for swimming.

Playa el Tecolote. Spend a Sunday at Playa el Tecolote, 24 km (15 mi) north of La Paz, and you'll feel like you've experienced the Mexico of old. Families set up housekeeping along the soft sand, kids race after seagulls, and grandmothers lift their skirts to wade in blue water. Vendors rent beach chairs, umbrellas, kayaks, and small motorized boats, and a couple of restaurants serve fresh grilled snapper. The restaurants are usually open throughout the week, though they sometimes close on wintery days. Facilities include public restrooms, fire pits, and trash cans. Camping is permitted, but there are no hookups.

WHERE TO EAT

$–$$$ Fodor'sChoice★ ✕**Buffalo Bar-B-Q.** Carnivores head to this steak joint for fresh certified Angus beef burgers and steaks. Start with casserole Rockefeller (mussels, shrimp, crab meat, and scallops sautéed in spinach butter and fennel, with a touch of chardonnay and melted mozzarella cheese). The porterhouse and rib eye are the best steak choices; all meats are grilled over a wood-burning mesquite fire pit. Fresh fish dishes round out the menu for nonmeat lovers. ⊠*Madero 1420 E/5 De Mayo and Constitución, Centro* ☎612/128–8755 ▭*MC, V.*

$–$$$ ✕**La Mar y Peña.** The freshest, tastiest seafood cocktails, ★ ceviches, and clam tacos imaginable are served in this nautical restaurant crowded with locals. If you can come with friends, go for the *mariscada*, a huge platter of shellfish and fish for four. The shrimp albondigas (meatballs) soup has a hearty fish stock seasoned with cilantro, and the crab *ranchero* is a savory mix of crabmeat, onions, tomatoes, and capers. Portions are huge. ⊠*Calle 16 de Septiembre, between Isabel de la Catolica and Albañez, Centro* ☎612/122–9949 ▭*AE, MC, V.*

¢–$$ ✕**El Bismark II.** You've got to go a bit out of your way for a local home-style Mexican restaurant. Tuck into seafood cocktails, enormous grilled lobsters, or carne asada served with beans, guacamole, and homemade tortillas. Families settle down for hours at long wood tables, while waitresses divide their attention between patrons and soap operas on the TV above the bar. The desultory service is a drawback. A smaller Bismark, established in 1971, is on the malecón. ⊠*Av. Degollado and Calle Altamirano, Centro* ☎612/122–4854 ▭*MC, V.*

¢–$ ✕**El Cangrejo Loco.** A few sidewalk tables sit outside this
tiny family-run café; seats are hard to come by at lunch-
time. There's a long list of seafood cocktails: shrimp, crab,
and clams with lime, chilies, or soy sauce. Entrées include
a great quesadilla with cheese and crab, manta ray tacos,
and stuffed crab. ⊠*Paseo Obregón, between Bravo and
Ocampo, Malecón* ☎612/122–1359 ⊟*No credit cards.*

¢–$ ✕**Los Laurelles.** Locals and tourists alike fill up the tables
★ at this open-air eatery for the just-caught seafood. Favorite dishes include fish, shrimp, and octopus dipped in gar-
lic butter; shrimp in a chipotle sauce; and fish fillet in a
white sauce. The best time to go? Right at sunset. A giant
papier-maché lobster out front marks the entrance. ⊠*Alvaro Obregón and Salvatierra facing Malecón, Centro*
☎612/128–8532 ⊟*No credit cards.*

¢–$ ✕**La Pazta.** Locals who crave international fare rave about
this trattoria with a sleek black-and-white color scheme and
excellent homemade pastas and pizzas. Look for imported
cheeses and wines and bracing espresso. The adjacent café
serves imported Italian coffee and breakfast and lunch.
Both are at the Hotel Mediterrane, a small inn popular
with Europeans. ⊠*Allende 36, at Hotel Mediterrane, Centro* ☎612/125–1195 ⊟*AE, MC, V* ⊙*No dinner Tues.*

¢–$ ✕**Taco Hermanos Gonzalez.** La Paz has plenty of great taco
★ stands, but the Gonzalez brothers still corner the market
with their hunks of fresh fish wrapped in corn tortillas.
Bowls of condiments line the small stand, and the top quality draws crowds of sidewalk munchers. ⊠*Mutualismo and
Esquerro, Centro* ☎*No phone* ⊟*No credit cards.*

¢ ✕**El Quinto Sol Restaurante Vegetariano.** El Quinto's brightly
painted exterior is covered with snake symbols and smil-
ing suns. The all-vegetarian menu includes fresh juices and
herbal elixirs. The four-course prix-fixe *comida corrida*
(daily special) is a bargain; it's served from noon to 4. The
back half of the space is a bare-bones natural-foods store.
⊠*Belisario Domínguez and Av. Independencia, Centro*
☎612/122–1692 ⊟*No credit cards.*

WHERE TO STAY

$$–$$$$ ▣**La Concha Beach Resort.** On a long beach with calm water,
☾ this older resort has a water-sports center and a notably
good restaurant. Rooms can be dark and uninviting, but
are gradually being renovated with white walls and cheery

yellow and blue textiles. If you can, splurge on a condo unit with separate bedroom and kitchen. There's an infrequent shuttle to town. ⊠*Carretera a Pichilingue, Km 5, between downtown and Pichilingue, 23010* ☎*612/121–6344, 800/999–2252 in U.S.* ⊕*www.laconcha.com* ⤵*107 rooms* ⚐*In-room: refrigerator. In-hotel: restaurant, bars, pool, beachfront, diving, water sports, laundry service, public Internet, no elevator* ⊟*AE, MC, V.*

$$$ ✕⊡**Posada De Las Flores.** Brightly painted walls, dark-wood
★ furnishings (handcrafted specially for the inn by master craftsmen from Tonala, Guadalajara), and wrought iron decorations make this small, hacienda-style inn facing the malecón both cozy and classy. Rooms have good views of La Paz bay; all-marble bathrooms have large bathtubs and thick terry towels. There's a small pool in the elegant courtyard. Café Las Flores, on the second level, has coffee, cappuccino, pastries, and ice cream. The inn provides kayaks, bicycles, and wireless Internet at no charge. Everything in town is within walking distance. ⊠*Alvaro Obregón 440, 23000* ☎*612/125–5871, 619/378–0103 in U.S.* ⊕*www. posadadelasflores.com* ⤵*5 rooms, 2 suites, 1 master suite* ⚐*In-room: minibar. In-hotel: restaurant, bar, no elevator, Wi-Fi* ⊟*MC, V* ⦿*BP.*

$$ ⊡**el angel azul.** Owner Esther Ammann converted La Paz's
★ historic courthouse into a bed-and-breakfast that's a comfortable retreat in the center of the city. Rooms frame a central courtyard filled with palms and bougainvillea. Walls throughout are painted vivid yellow, coral, and blue and are decorated with original art. The rooftop suite, which overlooks the city, is a guest favorite. ⊠*Av. Independencia 518, at Guillermo Prieto, Centro, 23000* ☎*612/125–5130* ⊕*www.elangelazul.com* ⤵*10 rooms, 1 suite* ⚐*In-room: no TV (some). In-hotel: bar, no kids under 12, no-smoking rooms, no elevator* ⊟*MC, V* ⦿*CP.*

$$ ⊡**Los Arcos.** This colonial-style 1950s hotel is a beloved La Paz landmark. The lobby leads to the courtyard, where the rush of water in the fountain drowns out street noise. Most rooms have balconies, some facing the bay (street noise is a drawback). The Cabañas de los Arcos next door consist of several small brick cottages surrounded by gardens and a small hotel with a pool. ⊠*Paseo Obregón 498, between Rosales and Allende, Malecón, 23000* ☎*612/122–2744, 800/347–2252 in U.S.* ⊕*www.losarcos. com* ⤵*93 rooms, 15 suites at hotel; 24 bungalows, 23*

9

rooms at Cabañas &*In-room: minibar. In-hotel: restaurant, bar, pools* =*AE, MC, V.*

$$ *Hotel Villa Marina.* Gardens surround the pool and Jacuzzi, and a seaside promenade lines the property. The full-service marina offers fishing, scuba diving, and kayaking. Private charters are available. Most rooms have terraces or balconies with water views. Naturally, it's popular with boaters sailing the Sea of Cortez; they share tales and tips at the Dinghy Dock restaurant. ⊠*Carretera a Pichilingue, Km 2.5, 23000* ☎*612/121–6254, 800/826–1138 in U.S.* ⊕*www.hotelmarina.com.mx* ⌖*86 rooms, 5 suites* &*In-hotel: restaurant, bar, tennis court, pool* =*AE, MC, V.*

$$ *La Perla.* The brown low-rise faces the malecón and has been a center of activity since 1940. Rooms have white walls and light-wood furnishings; some have king-size beds. The pool is on a second-story sundeck, away from main street traffic. Noise is a factor in the oceanfront rooms; the trade-off is wonderful sunset views. ⊠*Paseo Obregón 1570, Malecón, 23010* ☎*612/122–0777, 888/242–3757 in U.S.* ⊕*www.hotelperlabaja.com* ⌖*110 rooms* &*In-room: minibar. In-hotel: restaurant, bar, pool* =*AE, MC, V.*

$-$$ *La Casa Mexicana Inn.* Arlaine Cervantes has created a lovely homelike ambience in her small B&B just one block from the malecón. The rooms are decorated in calming pastels and have lots of niches and shelves with folk art. Some rooms overlook the bay, while others face the peaceful garden. Guests rave about the breakfasts. Some rooms have kitchenettes. ⊠*Calle Nicolas Bravo 106, Centro, 23000* ☎*612/125–2748* ⊕*www.casamex.com* ⌖*5 rooms* &*In-room: no phone, no TV. In-hotel: public Wi-Fi, no elevator* =*No credit cards.*

$-$$ *Hotel Suites Club El Moro.* A vacation-ownership resort with suite rentals on a nightly and weekly basis, El Moro has a palm-filled garden and a densely landscaped pool area. You can recognize the building by its stark-white turrets and domes. Rooms are Mediterranean in style, with arched windows, Mexican tiles, and private balconies. Some rooms have kitchens and can sleep up to five people. A small café serves breakfast and lunch. Fishing packages are available. ⊠*Carretera a Pichilingue, Km 2, between downtown and Pichilingue, 23010* ☎*612/122–4084* ⊕*www.clubelmoro.com* ⌖*26 suites* &*In-hotel: restaurant, bar, pool, no elevator* =*AE, MC, V* ⦿*CP.*

¢ ✕▣**Hotel Yeneka.** It may be quirky (a toy monkey at the wheel of an antiquated, rusted Model-T greets you as you enter the tropical courtyard), but it's a perfect bargain for clean rooms with bathrooms and showers. You can pay a bit more ($39–$42 per night) for some extra perks: laundry service, coffee in the morning, two shots of tequila at night, and Internet service. Ask owner Dr. Miguel Macias about the Menqeleluel Indian artwork that adorns the walls in every room. Kayak, bicycle, and snorkel gear are available for rental and the hotel can arrange diving and snorkeling excursions. Expect to rub shoulders with the backpacker crowd here. ✉*Madero 1520/16 de Septiembre, Centro* ☎612/125–4688 ✑ynkmacias@prodigy.net.mx ⇝*20 rooms* ⌂*In-room: no phone, no TV, no a/c (some). In-hotel: restaurant, bar, no elevator, Internet service* ▭*No credit cards.*

¢ ▣**Pensión California.** Few budget hotels in Baja feel like those on the mainland. This one has that edgy, almost unacceptable style beloved by those who travel rough. You can nab a bed here for less than $20; although the hacienda is run-down, the blue-and-white rooms have baths and are clean. The courtyard has picnic tables and a TV. ✉*Av. Degollado 209, Centro, 23000* ☎612/122–2896 ⇝*25 rooms* ⌂*In-room: no a/c, no TV. In-hotel: no elevator* ▭*No credit cards.*

NIGHTLIFE & THE ARTS

★ **El Teatro de la Ciudad** (✉*Av. Navarro 700, Centro* ☎612/125–0486) is La Paz's cultural center. The theater seats 1,500 and stages shows by visiting and local performers. **La Terraza** (✉*La Perla hotel, Paseo Obregón 1570, Malecón* ☎612/122–0777) is the best spot for both sunset- and people-watching along the malecón. The hotel also has a disco on weekends. **Las Varitas** (✉*Calle Independencia 111, Centro* ☎612/125–2025 ⊕*www.lasvaritas.com*), a Mexican rock club, heats up after midnight.

SHOPPING

Artesanías la Antigua California (✉*Paseo Obregón 220, Malecón* ☎612/125–5230) has the nicest selection of Mexican folk art in La Paz, including wooden masks and lacquered boxes from Guerrero. It also has a good supply of English-language books on Baja. **Artesanía Cuauhtémoc**

(⊠*Av. Abasolo between Calles Nayarit and Oaxaca, south of downtown, Centro* ☎612/122–4575) is the workshop of weaver Fortunado Silva, who creates and sells cotton place mats, rugs, and tapestries.

★ Julio Ibarra oversees the potters and painters at **Ibarra's Pottery** (⊠*Calle Prieto 625, Centro* ☎612/122–0404). His geometric designs and glazing technique result in gorgeous mirrors, bowls, platters, and cups. There's unusual pottery at **Mexican Designs** (⊠*Calle Arreola 41, at Av. Zaragoza, Centro* ☎612/123–2231). The boxes with cactus designs are particularly good souvenirs.

La Tiendita (⊠*Malecón, Centro* ☎612/125–2744) has embroidered guayabera shirts and dresses, tin ornaments and picture frames, and black pottery from Oaxaca. You can pop into an outdoor eatery along the block-long **municipal market** (⊠*Calle Serdan and Ocampo*), or just stroll the street for Mexican arts and crafts, fresh produce, nuts, and meats.

ACTIVITIES

BOATING & FISHING

The considerable fleet of private boats in La Paz now has room for docking at four marinas: Fidepaz Marina at the north end of town, the Marina Palmira and Marina La Paz south of town, and Marina Costa Baja, at Km 7.5 on the La Paz–Pichilingue Road. Most hotels can arrange trips. Tournaments are held in August, September, and October. The **Mosquito Fleet** (⊠*La Paz–Pichilingue Rd., Km 5* ☎612/121–6120 *or* 877/408–6769) has cabin cruisers with charters starting around $550 for up to four people, deluxe super *pangas* (skiffs) at $350 for three people, and super *pangas* at $220 for two people. They also offer dive and snorkeling excursions.

DIVING & SNORKELING

Popular diving and snorkeling spots include the coral banks off Isla Espíritu Santo, the sea-lion colony off Isla Partida, and the seamount 14 km (9 mi) farther north (best for serious divers).

Baja Expeditions (⊠*2625 Garnet Ave., San Diego, CA 92109* ☎858/581–3311 *or* 800/843–6967 ⊕*www.bajaex. com*) runs daylong and multiday dive packages in the Sea of Cortez. Packages start at about $375 per person (double occupancy) for a three-night, two-day diving package.

Seven-day excursions aboard the 80-foot *Don José* dedicated dive boat start at $1,445 for cabin, food, and nearly unlimited diving. Live-aboard trips run from May into October. You may spot whale sharks in May and June.

★ The **Cortez Club** (⊠*La Concha Beach Resort, Carretera a Pichilingue, Km 5, between downtown and Pichilingue* ☎*612/121–6120 or 612/121–6121* ⊕*www.cortezclub.com*) is a full-scale water-sports center with equipment rental and scuba, snorkeling, kayaking, and sportfishing tours. A two-tank dive costs about $110. **Fun Baja** (⊠*Carretera a Pichilingue, Km 2* ☎*612/121–5884* ⊕*www.funbaja.com*) offers scuba and snorkel trips with the sea lions. Scuba trips start at $130.

KAYAKING

★ The calm waters off La Paz are perfect for kayaking, and you can take multiday trips along the coast to Loreto or out to the nearby islands. **Baja Expeditions** (⊠*2625 Garnet Ave., San Diego, CA 92109* ☎*858/581–3311 or 800/843–6967* ⊕*www.bajaex.com*), one of the oldest outfitters working in Baja, offers several kayak tours, including multinight trips between Loreto and La Paz. A support boat carries all the gear, including ingredients for great meals. The seven-day trip with camping on remote island beaches starts at $1,045 per person.

Baja Quest (⊠*Sonora 174, Centro* ☎*612/123–5320*) has day and overnight kayak trips. Day trips cost about $90 per person. **Fun Baja** (⊠*Carretera a Pichilingue, Km 2* ☎*612/121–5884* ⊕*www.funbaja.com*) offers kayak trips around the islands, scuba and snorkel excursions, and land tours. A day of kayaking and snorkeling will run about $100. **Nichols Expeditions** (⊠*497 N. Main, Moab, UT 84532* ☎*435/259–3999 or 800/648–8488* ⊕*www.nicholsexpeditions.com*) arranges kayaking tours to Isla Espíritu Santo and between Loreto and La Paz, with camping along the way. A nine-day trip costs $1,300.

WHALE-WATCHING

La Paz is a good entry point for whale-watching expeditions to Bahía Magdalena, 266 km (165 mi) northwest of La Paz on the Pacific coast. Note, however, that such trips entail about six hours of travel from La Paz and back for two to three hours on the water. Only a few tour companies offer this as a daylong excursion, however, because of the time and distance constraints.

Many devoted whale-watchers opt to stay overnight in San Carlos, the small town by the bay. Most La Paz hotels can make arrangements for excursions, or you can head out on your own by renting a car or taking a public bus from La Paz to San Carlos, and then hiring a boat captain to take you into the bay. The air and water are cold, so you'll need to bring a warm windbreaker and gloves. Captains must keep their boats away from the whales, who may approach so closely you can reach out and touch them.

An easier expedition is a whale-watching trip in the Sea of Cortez from La Paz, which involves boarding a boat in La Paz and sailing around until whales are spotted. They most likely won't come as close to the boats and you won't see the mothers and newborn calves at play, but it's still fabulous watching the whales breeching and spouting nearby.

Baja Expeditions (⊠ *2625 Garnet Ave., San Diego, CA92109* ☎ *858/581–3311 or 800/843–6967* ⊕ *www.bajaex.com*) runs seven-day trips from La Paz to Magdalena Bay, including boat trips, camping, and meals; prices start at $1,350 per person. The company also runs adventure cruises around the tip of Baja between La Paz and Magdalena Bay. The eight-day cruises start at $1,695 per person.

Trips including camping at Mag Bay, but not including airfare and hotel in La Paz, are available through **Baja Quest** (⊠ *Sonora 174, Centro* ☎ *612/123–5320* ⊕ *www.bajaquest. com.mx*). The two-night camping trip starts at $695 per person; the four-night trip starts at $1,050 per person. The water-sports center **Cortez Club** (⊠ *La Concha Beach Resort, Carretera a Pichilingue, Km 5, between downtown and Pichilingue* ☎ *612/121–6120 or 612/121–6121* ⊕ *www.cortezclub.com*) runs extremely popular whale-watching trips in winter. A day-trip, starting at 6 AM, costs $150 per person with a four-person minimum.

LA PAZ ESSENTIALS

Whether you come from Cabo San Lucas or San José del Cabo, La Paz is more than a two-hour drive, part of it through the mountains. It can make a nice day tour, as long as you don't spend too much time getting here and back. If you want to make lengthy stops, you are better off spending the night (⇨ *Where to Stay*).

BY BUS

To get to downtown La Paz from the main bus station, take any city bus and get off at the city market, or *mercado municipal* (Calle Revolución at Calle Degollado). To return, downtown city buses marked IMSS will let you off three blocks from the terminal. Águila buses to the beaches and ferry terminal in Pichilingue (10 a day, 20 minutes, $1) leave from **Terminal Malecón** (⊠*Av. Obregón* ☎*612/122–7898*). The last bus back to La Paz departs Pichilingue at 6 PM.

ABC and Águila buses arrive at the **main bus station** (⊠*Calle Jalisco at Calle Héroes de la Independencia* ☎*612/122– 4270*), a 30-minute walk or a $2.50 taxi ride from downtown. **Águila** (☎*612/122–7898*) has a stop at the north end of the malecón. Buses depart the Cabo San Lucas terminal for La Paz daily, every one to two hours, traveling via Todos Santos; the fare is $10 one-way. Buses from San José del Cabo leave from the Águila terminal just off Highway 1 and pass Buena Vista and Los Barriles; the fare to La Paz is $10.

BY CAR

From San José del Cabo, take the Transpeninsular Highway (Hwy. 1). From San Lucas take Highway 19, which joins Highway 1 after Todos Santos. Or, better yet, drive up on scenic Highway 1 and back on Highway 19. Stay on the paved highways; roads are narrow and without lights, and cows and other animals roam freely. You may have to stop for road repairs during and after the rainy season.

BY VAN TOUR

Full-day van tours from Los Cabos to La Paz cost about $75 per person, including breakfast, snacks, and drinks. Ask for an itinerary beforehand, as some guides simply drop you off on the malecón and pick you up about three hours later. **Contactours** (⊠*Av. Zaragoza at 5 de Febrero, San José del Cabo* ☎*624/143–2439*) will provide a van and guide for private tours to La Paz. **Rancho Tours** (⊠*Libertad, at 20 de Noviembre, Cabo San Lucas* ☎*624/143– 5464*) also has full-day van tours to La Paz. **Transcabo Tours** (⊠*Hwy. 1, Km 43 San José del Cabo* ☎*624/146–0888*) has tours to La Paz.

9

BUENA VISTA & LOS BARRILES

Buena Vista: 32 km (20 mi) north of San José del Cabo;
Los Barriles: 34 km (21 mi) north of San José del Cabo.

The Sea of Cortez coast between La Paz and San José del
Cabo is a favored hideaway for anglers and adventurers.
The area by San José, dubbed the East Cape, consists of
several fast-growing settlements including Cabo Pulmo,
Buena Vista, Los Barriles, and Punta Pescadero. The East
Cape is renowned for its rich fishing grounds, good diving,
and excellent windsurfing. Most hotels *(⇨ Where to Stay)*
offer packages that include meals and activities. The East
Cape makes a good day trip or a nice place to overnight,
especially if you're into water sports.

Intrepid travelers can drive north on a dirt washboard road
to the East Cape settlements, then return on the paved
Highway 1. This route is *not* recommended for those both-
ered by dust or long stretches of precipitous driving conditions; some car rental agencies do not allow their cars on
these roads. Stop along the way to snorkel or dive in Cabo
Pulmo or windsurf in Los Barriles. If you want to fish this
part of the Sea of Cortez, plan on spending a night so you
can be out on the water in early morning. You can rent
water-sports equipment and organize boat trips through
area hotels.

SIGHTS TO SEE

The East Cape is more about activities than attractions.
Whether you drive the dirt road or highway, you'll find
plenty of places to stop and play or simply admire the scenery. The following places are worth exploring as you work
your way north from San José.

Divers and snorkelers need go no farther than **Cabo Pulmo**,
site of one of the few coral reefs in the Sea of Cortez. You
can dive with one of the shops in the area or just slip on
your mask and snorkel and swim about admiring the
tropical fish. The reef is part of a national marine reserve,
and you may not remove anything from the water. Rustic
stands on the beach sell food and drinks.

Vacationers and expat settlers are drawn to **Buena Vista,**
which has more services and infrastructure than the
East Cape's more remote outposts. You can sign up for

fishing and diving excursions at the Hotel Buena Vista Beach Resort.

Atop the flat crest of La Bandera mountain stands an elaborate, towering **concrete flagpole.** The memorial honors Mexico's flag and is the site of the Día de la Bandera (Day of the Flag) fiesta, which takes place February 24. The fiesta emerged as a kind of cultural-pride response to the growing American influence in the area in the 1950s. To reach the memorial, take the dirt road that winds up through the rocks near the Buena Vista turnoff from Highway 1.

La Bandera mountain affords spectacular views of **Bahía de Palmas** *(Bay of Palms)*, one of the most beautiful coves on the Sea of Cortez. Many of the East Cape's resorts face the bay. Windsurfers are drawn by the fierce winds during the winter months. **Vela Windsurf** (☎ *800/223–5443 in U.S.* ⊕ *www.velawindsurf.com*) arranges multiday windsurfing trips based at East Cape hotels from November through mid-March. Las Palmas Bay is 77 km (48 mi) north of San José on Highway 1; turn off at the Buena Vista sign.

WHERE TO EAT

¢–$$ ✕**Nancy's Restaurant & Bar.** Don't let the plain-Jane plastic tables and chairs of this little find fool you; Nancy's a graduate of the famed Cordon Bleu in Paris, and her culinary talents stun the palate. You can bring in your day's catch for her to prepare, or let her know in advance that you want to dine for dinner—she'll tailor a menu at her discretion. Nancy's also serves breakfast, pizza, tacos, homemade breads, and soups. ✉ *Near Cabo Pulmo Resort in town center* ☎ *No phone* ▭ *No credit cards.*

¢–$$ ✕**Otra Vez.** If you're ready for grilled fish or a burger by the time you reach Los Barriles, stop at this great little California-style café. The clientele consists largely of expat retirees and tourists who gossip freely while listening to the Beach Boys or occasional live music. ✉ *Calle 20 de Noviembre, Los Barriles* ☎ *612/142–0249* ▭ *MC, V.*

¢–$ ✕**Tia Licha.** A good, solid place to start your day is at this tiny café known for its home-style cooking and fresh fish. Locals congregate here for what is said to be the best breakfast on the East Cape. ✉ *On road to Hotel Buena Vista Beach Resort, Buena Vista* ☎ *No phone* ▭ *No credit cards.*

WHERE TO STAY

$$$–$$$$ ☒ **Rancho Leonero Resort.** Settle in here for seclusion and
★ striking views of the Sea of Cortez: rock-walled, palapa-
roofed rooms all overlook the water. Though it's on a rocky
point, the 5 km (3 mi) of deserted sandy beach are perfect
for sunning. Don your snorkeling gear and head out front to
the hotel's double-reef to explore the variety of multicolor
marine life. The sport-fishing fleet has super *pangas* start-
ing at $250 per day and cruisers at $385 per day. Scuba,
kayaking, and horseback riding trips are also available.
⊠*Off Km 103 on Mexico Hwy. 1* ⌂*1560 N. Coast Hwy.,
Luecadia, CA 92024* ☎*612/241–0216 or 760/634–4336,
800/646–2252 in U.S.* ⊕*www.rancholeonero.com* ⤳*34
rooms* ⌂*In-room: no TV, no phone. In hotel: restaurant,
bar, pool, public Wi-Fi* ⊟*MC, V* ⦿*AI.*

$$–$$$ ☒ **Hotel Buena Vista Beach Resort.** Tile-roof bungalows sit
☼ along flower-lined paths next to pools, fountains, and
lawns. Some rooms have private terraces. The fishing fleet
is excellent, as are other diversions, such as diving, snor-
keling, kayaking, horseback riding, and trips to natural
springs. Hot springs run underneath the hotel; the water
is cooled and pumped through the hotel. A European
plan (without meals) is available from November through
March, which cuts the rate considerably. The food is decent.
⊠*Carretera 1, Km 105, Buena Vista, 23500* ☎*624/141–
0033 or 619/429–8079, 800/752–3555 in U.S.* ⊕*www.
hotelbuenavista.com* ⤳*60 rooms* ⌂*In-room: no phone, no
TV. In-hotel: restaurant, tennis court, pools, beachfront,
water sports, no elevator* ⊟*MC, V* ⦿*FAP.*

$$$ ☒ **Hotel Palmas de Cortez.** The Palmas is the East Cape's
social center. Often featured on sportfishing shows, the
hotel is near the famed Cortez Banks and has its own fleet.
Its enormous pool has a swim-up bar, and a full spa pam-
pers anglers and their companions. Swedish, therapeutic,
sports, and aromatherapy massages go for $80 an hour
and $115 for an hour and a half. Some guest rooms have
fireplaces and/or kitchens, and there's also a nine-hole
golf course and driving range. Special events, including
an arts festival in March and several fishing tournaments,
are big draws. ⊠*On the beach; take road north through
Los Barriles and continue to beach, Los Barriles* ⌂*Box
9016, Calabasas, CA 91372* ☎*624/141–0214, 877/777–
8862 in U.S.* ⊕*www.palmasdecortez.com* ⤳*35 rooms, 15
suites, 10 condos* ⌂*In-hotel: restaurant, golf course, tennis*

court, pool, gym, spa, public Internet, no elevator ⊟*MC,
V* ⊚*FAP.*

¢–$$$ ⊞**Cabo Pulmo Beach Resort.** Solar-powered cottages sit in even
rows on the beach, much like in a trailer park. Owners put
their vacation homes up for rent through this back-to-basics
resort. The office is next to a PADI facility and a restaurant.
It's the largest business in the neighborhood and the best
place for newcomers to hang out for a few nights. The set-
ting is idyllic. ⊠*Hwy. 1 at La Ribera turnoff, Cabo Pulmo*
☎*624/141–0244* ⊚*www.cabopulmo.com* ⌂*In-room: no a/
c, no phone, kitchen (some), refrigerator (some), no TV. In-
hotel: restaurant, beachfront, diving, water sports, no eleva-
tor* ⊟*MC, V.*

$–$$ ⊞**Los Barriles Hotel.** Across the street from beachside businesses, this motel-like inn offers comfy, large, simple rooms
at a great price. The two-story building wraps around a
central pool and lounging area; water and cold drinks are
available at the front desk, as are tours and fishing trips.
⊠*Take road off Hwy. 1 north through Los Barriles and
turn left when it ends at beach, Los Barriles* ☎☎*624/141–
0024* ⊚*www.losbarrileshotel.com* ⇆*20 rooms* ⌂*In-room:
no TV. In-hotel: pool, no elevator* ⊟*MC, V.*

ACTIVITIES

Water-sports equipment and boat trips are available
through area hotels, although regulars tend to bring their
own gear and rent cars to reach isolated spots. Windsurfers take over the East Cape in winter, when stiff breezes
provide ideal conditions. Catch them flying over the waves
at Playa Norte in Los Barriles. **VelaWindsurf** (☎*800/223–
5443 in U.S.* ⊚*www.velawindsurf.com*) offers windsurfing
and kite-boarding lessons and trips to Los Barriles from
November to March.

After the summer rains, rent an ATV and head out to some
of the nearby arroyos while streams of water still trickle
down from the Sierra De La Laguna Mountain Range; we
think the most thrilling ride is to the Buenos Aires Arroyo
Waterfall. **Quadman** (⊠*Main St., Los Barriles center*
☎*624/141–0727*) rents new Yamaha automatic ATVs at
$50 for three hours and $100 for 24 hours.

9

SHOPPING

The **Plaza Del Pueblo** (⊠*Carretera 1, Los Barriles*) is the area's most complete shopping opportunity. The small center includes a friendly restaurant-bar, an Internet café, a gym, a realty office (of course), and an excellent shop with postcards, Baja books, and desirable souvenirs.

NIGHTLIFE

Nightlife is in short supply here. **Tio Pablo's** (☎*612/142–1214*) is your standard fully stocked bar, with satellite sports TV and bar fare such as burgers and salads. It's nothing fancy, but it's a decent place to enjoy a cold one. (To get here, take the main road in town [no name] toward the beach until it dead ends and turn left.)

BUENA VISTA & LOS BARRILES ESSENTIALS

Along Highway 1, Buena Vista is 75 km (47 mi) and Los Barriles 77 km (48 mi) north of San José. Travel during the week if possible, as weekends can be crowded.

The simplest way to visit these neighboring towns in one day is to rent a car. You can reach several beaches easily, but to navigate most dirt roads safely—including the rough Coastal Road—you need a four-wheel-drive vehicle with high ground clearance. Get a good map that shows off-road routes. The cape's more courteous drivers turn on their left-turn signal to indicate that you may pass them. Watch closely, though. The driver may actually be turning left.

You can also arrange van tours to the East Cape from Los Cabos. Prices run about $65 for a full-day van tour. **Rancho Tours** (⊠*Libertad, at 20 de Noviembre, Cabo San Lucas* ☎*624/143–5464*) offers ATV tours on the East Cape; call for details and prices. **Transcabo Tours** (⊠*Hwy. 1, Km 43 San José del Cabo* ☎*624/146–0888*) runs van tours to Cabo Pulmo.

Los Cabos Essentials

PLANNING TOOLS, EXPERT INSIGHT, GREAT CONTACTS

There are planners and there are those who, excuse the pun, fly by the seat of their pants. We happily place ourselves among the planners. Our writers and editors try to anticipate all the issues you may face before and during any journey, and then they do their research. This section is the product of their efforts. Use it to get excited about your trip to Los Cabos, to inform your travel planning, or to guide you on the road should the seat of your pants start to feel threadbare.

GETTING STARTED

We're really proud of our Web site: Fodors.com is a great place to begin any journey. Scan Travel Wire for suggested itineraries, travel deals, restaurant and hotel openings, and other up-to-the-minute info. Check out Booking to research prices and book plane tickets, hotel rooms, rental cars, and vacation packages. Head to Talk for on-the-ground pointers from travelers who frequent our message boards. You can also link to loads of other travel-related resources.

RESOURCES

ONLINE TRAVEL TOOLS

ALL ABOUT LOS CABOS

The best information about ecotourism and environmental issues is at *www.planeta.com*. Discover Baja, a membership club for Baja travelers, has links and info at *www.discoverbaja.com*. Links to Los Cabos businesses and other information are available at *www.bajalife.com*, *www.baja-web.com*, and *www.loscabosguide.com*.

Currency Conversion Google (⊕www.google.com) does currency conversion. Just type in the amount you want to convert and an explanation of how you want it converted (e.g., "14 Swiss francs in dollars"), and then voilà. **Oanda.com** (⊕www.oanda.com) also allows you to print out a handy table with the current day's conversion rates.

XE.com (⊕www.xe.com) is a good currency conversion Web site.

Safety Transportation Security Administration (TSA; ⊕www.tsa.gov).

Time Zones Timeanddate.com (⊕www.timeanddate.com/worldclock) can help you figure out the correct time anywhere.

Weather Accuweather.com (⊕www.accuweather.com) is an independent weather-forecasting service with good coverage of hurricanes. **Weather.com** (⊕www.weather.com) is the Web site for the Weather Channel.

Other Resources CIA World Factbook (⊕www.odci.gov/cia/publications/factbook/index.html) has profiles of every country in the world. It's a good source if you need some quick facts and figures.

VISITOR INFORMATION

The Mexican-government tourist office and the private travel sector have joined together to form a national tourist and promotion board, so the best way to get information is via the toll-free number that connects you to the promotion office in Mexico City (operators speak English). The Los Cabos municipal government created a tourism office in 2003; at this writing, their offices had not yet opened to the public, but you can reach staff by phone or get information online. Otherwise, your hotel tour desk is always a good source. Avoid tour stands on the streets; they're usually associated with time-share operations.

Contacts **Los Cabos Tourism Board** (☎866/567–2226 ⊕www.visitcabo.com). **Mexican Government Tourist & Promotion Board** (☎800/446–3942 from U.S. and Canada ⊕www.visitmexico.com).

▌THINGS TO CONSIDER

GOVERNMENT ADVISORIES

As different countries have different worldviews, look at travel advisories from a range of governments to get more of a sense of what's going on out there. And be sure to parse the language carefully. For example, a warning to "avoid all travel" carries more weight than one urging you to "avoid nonessential travel," and both are much stronger than a plea to "exercise caution." A U.S. government travel warning is more permanent (though not necessarily more serious) than a so-called public announcement, which carries an expiration date.

▌TIP→ Consider registering online with the State Department (https://travelregistration.state.gov/ibrs/), so the government will know to look for you should a crisis occur in the country you're visiting.

The U.S. Department of State's Web site has more than just travel warnings and advisories. The consular information sheets issued for every country have general safety tips, entry requirements (though be sure to verify these with the country's embassy), and other useful details.

General Information & Warnings
Australian Department of Foreign Affairs & Trade (⊕www.smartraveller.gov.au). **Consular Affairs Bureau of Canada** (⊕www.voyage.gc.ca). **U.K. Foreign & Commonwealth Office** (⊕www.fco.gov.uk/travel). **U.S. Department of State** (⊕www.travel.state.gov).

GEAR

SHIPPING LUGGAGE AHEAD Imagine globe-trotting with only a carry-on in tow. Shipping your luggage in advance via an air-freight service is a great way to cut down on backaches, hassles, and stress—especially if your packing list includes strollers, car seats, etc. There are some things to be aware of, though.

First, research carry-on restrictions; if you absolutely need something that isn't practical to ship and isn't allowed in carry-ons, this strategy isn't for you. Second, plan to send your bags several days in advance to U.S. destinations and as much as two weeks in advance to some international destinations. Third, plan to spend some money: it will cost at least $100 to send a small piece of luggage, a golf bag, or a pair of skis to a domestic destination, much more to places overseas.

Some people use Federal Express to ship their bags, but this can cost even more than air-freight services. All these services insure your bag (for most, the limit is $1,000, but you should verify that amount); you can, however, purchase additional insurance for about $1 per $100 of value.

Contacts **Luggage Concierge** (☎800/288-9818 ⊕www.lug-gageconcierge.com). **Luggage Express** (☎866/744-7224 ⊕www.usxpluggageexpress.com). **Luggage Free** (☎800/361-6871 ⊕www.luggagefree.com). **Sports Express** (☎800/357-4174 ⊕www.sportsexpress.com) specializes in shipping golf clubs and other sports equipment. **Virtual Bellhop** (☎877/235-5467 ⊕www.virtualbellhop.com).

PASSPORTS & VISAS
A tourist card is required for all Americans traveling to Mexico, and if arriving by air, Americans must also carry a valid passport. Minors traveling with one parent need notarized permission from the absent parent. You'll be given a tourist card application form on your flight; the cost of around $20 is usually included in the price of your airline ticket. You're supposed to keep a portion of the form. Be sure that you do. You'll be asked to hand it, your ticket, and your passport to airline representatives at the gate when boarding for departure. Not having your

tourist-visa documentation will be a problem.

PASSPORTS
A passport verifies both your identity and nationality—a great reason to have one. Another reason is that you need a passport now more than ever. At this writing, U.S. citizens must have a passport when traveling by air between the United States and several destinations for which other forms of identification (e.g., a driver's license and a birth certificate) were once sufficient. These destinations include Mexico, Canada, Bermuda, and all countries in Central America and the Caribbean (except the territories of Puerto Rico and the U.S. Virgin Islands). Soon enough you'll need a passport when traveling between the United States and such destinations by land and sea, too.

U.S. passports are valid for 10 years. You must apply in person if you're getting a passport for the first time; if your previous passport was lost, stolen, or damaged; or if your previous passport has expired and was issued more than 15 years ago or when you were under 16. All children under 18 must appear in person to apply for or renew a passport. Both parents must accompany any child under 14 (or send a notarized statement with their permission) and provide proof of their relationship to the child.

■TIP→ Before your trip, make two copies of your passport's data

PACKING 101

Why do some people travel with a convoy of huge suitcases yet never have a thing to wear? How do others pack a duffle with a week's worth of outfits *and* supplies for every contingency?

Make a list. You can use your list to pack and to repack at the end of your trip. It can also serve as a record of the contents of your suitcase—in case it disappears in transit.

Think it through. What's the weather like? Is this a business trip? In some places dress may be more or less conservative than you're used to. As you create your itinerary, note outfits next to each activity (don't forget accessories).

Edit your wardrobe. Plan to wear everything twice (better yet, thrice) and to do laundry along the way. Stick to one basic look—urban chic, sporty casual, etc. Build around one or two neutrals and an accent (e.g., black, white, and olive green). For a week's trip, you can look smashing with three bottoms, four or five tops, a sweater, and a jacket.

Be practical. Put comfortable shoes atop your list. Pack lightweight, wrinkle-resistent, compact, washable items. Stack and roll clothes, so they'll wrinkle less. Finally, select luggage you can readily carry. Porters, like good butlers, are hard to find these days.

Check weight and size limitations. You may be charged extra for checked bags weighing more than 50 pounds, or your airline may simply not allow bags that are heavier than this, or you may be charged a hefty fee for overweight baggage.

Check carry-on restrictions. Research restrictions with the TSA. Rules vary abroad, so check them with your airline if you're traveling overseas on a foreign carrier. Nevertheless, never pack essentials (travel documents, prescription meds, wallet) in checked luggage.

Rethink valuables. On U.S. flights, airlines are liable for only about $2,800 per person for bags. On international flights, the liability limit is around $635 per bag. But items like computers, cameras, and jewelry aren't covered at all. Your home-owner's policy may cover you sufficiently when you travel—or not.

Lock it up. If you must pack valuables, use TSA-approved locks (about $10) that can be unlocked by all U.S. security personnel.

Tag it. Always tag your luggage; use your business address if you don't want your home address visible outside your bag. Put the same information (and a copy of your itinerary) inside your luggage, too.

Report problems immediately. If your bags—or things in them—are damaged or go astray, file a written claim with your airline *before leaving the airport*. Most bags are found within 48 hours, but ask the airline if you can get a small allowance to purchase essentials.

page (one for someone at home and another for you to carry separately). Or scan the page and e-mail it to someone at home and/or yourself.

There are 13 regional passport offices, as well as 7,000 passport acceptance facilities in post offices, public libraries, and other governmental offices. If you're renewing a passport, you can do so by mail. Forms are available at passport acceptance facilities and online.

The cost to apply for a new passport is $97 for adults, $82 for children under 16; renewals are $67. Allow six weeks for processing, both for first-time passports and renewals. For an expediting fee of $60 you can reduce this time to about two weeks. If your trip is less than two weeks away, you can get a passport even more rapidly by going to a passport office with the necessary documentation. Private expediters can get things done in as little as 48 hours, but charge hefty fees for their services.

VISAS

A visa is essentially formal permission to enter a country. Visas allow countries to keep track of you and other visitors—and generate revenue (from application fees). You *always* need a visa to enter a foreign country; however, many countries routinely issue tourist visas on arrival, particularly to U.S. citizens. When your passport is stamped or scanned in the immigration line, you're actually being issued

a visa. Sometimes you have to stand in a separate line and pay a small fee to get your stamp before going through immigration, but you can still do this at the airport on arrival.

Getting a visa isn't always that easy. Some countries require that you arrange for one in advance of your trip. There's usually—but not always—a fee involved, and said fee may be nominal ($10 or less) or substantial ($100 or more).

If you must apply for a visa in advance, you can usually do it in person or by mail. When you apply by mail, you send your passport to a designated consulate, where your passport will be examined and the visa issued. Expediters—usually the same ones who handle expedited passport applications—can do all the work of obtaining your visa for you; however, there's always an additional cost (often more than $50 per visa).

Most visas limit you to a single trip—basically during the actual dates of your planned vacation. Other visas allow you to visit as many times as you wish for a specific period of time. Remember that requirements change, sometimes at the drop of a hat, and the burden is on you to make sure that you have the appropriate visas. Otherwise, you'll be turned away at the airport or, worse, deported after you arrive in the country. No company or travel insurer gives refunds if your travel plans are disrupted because you didn't have the correct visa.

U.S. Passport Information

U.S. Department of State
(☎877/487–2778 ⊕http://travel.state.gov/passport).

U.S. Passport & Visa Expediters **A. Briggs Passport & Visa Expediters** (☎800/806–0581 or 202/338–0111 ⊕www.abriggs.com). **American Passport Express** (☎800/455–5166 or 800/841–6778 ⊕www.americanpassport.com). **Passport Express** (☎800/362–8196 ⊕www.passportexpress.com). **Travel Document Systems** (☎800/874–5100 or 202/638–3800 ⊕www.traveldocs.com). **Travel the World Visas** (☎866/886–8472 or 301/495–7700 ⊕www.world-visa.com).

GENERAL REQUIREMENTS FOR MEXICO	
Passport	Must be valid for period of travel.
Visa	Tourist card required for Americans ($20, usually included in airline ticket)
Vaccinations	None required
Driving	U.S. driver's license accepted; Mexican auto insurance required.
Departure Tax	$10 (usually included in the airline ticket)

SHOTS & MEDICATIONS

According to the U.S. National Centers for Disease Control and Prevention (CDC), there's a limited risk of dengue fever and other insect-carried or parasite-caused illnesses in some rural parts of Mexico, though Baja California Sur is not one of the major areas of concern. *For more information see Health under On the Ground, below.*

■TIP→ **If you travel a lot internationally—particularly to developing nations—refer to the CDC's** *Health Information for International Travel* **(aka Traveler's Health Yellow Book). Info from it is posted on the CDC Web site (www.cdc.gov/travel/yb), or you can buy a copy from your local bookstore for $24.95.**

Health Warnings **National Centers for Disease Control & Prevention** (CDC ☎877/394–8747 international travelers' health line ⊕www.cdc.gov/travel). **World Health Organization** (WHO ⊕www.who.int).

TRIP INSURANCE

What kind of coverage do you honestly need? Do you need trip insurance at all? Take a deep breath and read on.

We believe that comprehensive trip insurance is especially valuable if you're booking a very expensive or complicated trip (particularly to an isolated region) or if you're booking far in advance. Who knows what could happen six months down the road? But whether you get insurance has more to do with how comfortable you are assuming all that risk yourself.

Comprehensive travel policies typically cover trip-cancellation and interruption, letting you cancel or cut your trip short because of a personal emergency, illness, or, in some cases, acts of terrorism in your destination. Such policies also cover evacuation and medical care. Some also cover you for trip delays because of bad weather or mechanical problems as well as for lost or delayed baggage. Another type of coverage to look for is financial default—that is, when your trip is disrupted because a tour operator, airline, or cruise line goes out of business. Generally you must buy this when you book your trip or shortly thereafter, and it's only available to you if your operator isn't on a list of excluded companies.

If you're going abroad, consider buying medical-only coverage at the very least. Neither Medicare nor some private insurers cover medical expenses anywhere outside of the United States (including time aboard a cruise ship, even if it leaves from a U.S. port). Medical-only policies typically reimburse you for medical care (excluding that related to preexisting conditions) and hospitalization abroad, and provide for evacuation. You still have to pay the bills and await reimbursement from the insurer, though.

Expect comprehensive travel insurance policies to cost about 4% to 7% or 8% of the total price of your trip (it's more like 8%–12% if you're over age 70). A medical-only policy may or may not be cheaper than a comprehensive policy. Always read the fine print of your policy to make sure that you are covered for the risks that are of most concern to you. Compare several policies to make sure you're getting the best price and range of coverage available.

■TIP→ OK. You know you can save a bundle on trips to warm-weather destinations by traveling in rainy season. But there's also a chance that a severe storm will disrupt your plans. The solution? Look for hotels and resorts that offer storm/hurricane guarantees. Although they rarely allow refunds, most guarantees do let you rebook later if a storm strikes.

Trip Insurance Resources

INSURANCE COMPARISON SITES		
Insure My Trip.com	800/487–4722	www.insuremytrip.com
Square Mouth.com	800/240–0369	www.quotetravelinsurance.com
Comprehensive Travel Insurers		
Access America	866/807–3982	www.accessamerica.com
CSA Travel Protection	800/873–9855	www.csatravelprotection.com
HTH Worldwide	610/254–8700 or 888/243–2358	www.hthworldwide.com
Travelex Insurance	888/457–4602	www.travelex-insurance.com
Travel Guard International	715/345–0505 or 800/826–4919	www.travelguard.com
Travel Insured International	800/243–3174	www.travelinsured.com
Medical-Only Insurers		
International Medical Group	800/628–4664	www.imglobal.com
International SOS	215/942–8000 or 713/521–7611	www.internationalsos.com
Wallach & Company	800/237–6615 or 504/687–3166	www.wallach.com

BOOKING YOUR TRIP

Unless your cousin is a travel agent, you're probably among the millions of people who make most of their travel arrangements online.

But have you ever wondered just what the differences are between an online travel agent (a Web site through which you make reservations instead of going directly to the airline, hotel, or car-rental company), a discounter (a firm that does a high volume of business with a hotel chain or airline and accordingly gets good prices), a wholesaler (one that makes cheap reservations in bulk and then resells them to people like you), and an aggregator (one that compares all the offerings so you don't have to)?

Is it truly better to book directly on an airline or hotel Web site? And when does a real live travel agent come in handy?

ONLINE

You really have to shop around. A travel wholesaler such as Hotels.com or HotelClub.net can be a source of good rates, as can discounters such as Hotwire or Priceline, particularly if you can bid for your hotel room or airfare. Indeed, such sites sometimes have deals that are unavailable elsewhere. They do, however, tend to work only with hotel chains (which makes them just plain useless for getting hotel reservations outside of major cities) or big airlines (so that often leaves out upstarts like jetBlue and some foreign carriers like Air India).

Also, with discounters and wholesalers you must generally prepay, and everything is nonrefundable. And before you fork over the dough, be sure to check the terms and conditions, so you know what a given company will do for you if there's a problem and what you'll have to deal with on your own.

■TIP→ **To be absolutely sure everything was processed correctly, confirm reservations made through online travel agents, discounters, and wholesalers directly with your hotel before leaving home.**

Booking engines like Expedia, Travelocity, and Orbitz are actually travel agents, albeit high-volume, online ones. And airline travel packagers like American Airlines Vacations and Virgin Vacations—well, they're travel agents, too. But they may still not work with all the world's hotels.

An aggregator site will search many sites and pull the best prices for airfares, hotels, and rental cars from them. Most aggregators compare the major travel-booking sites such as Expedia, Travelocity, and Orbitz; some also look at airline Web sites, though rarely the sites of smaller budget airlines. Some aggregators also compare other travel products, including complex packages—a good thing, as you can sometimes get the best overall deal by booking an air-and-hotel package.

▌ WITH A TRAVEL AGENT

If you use an agent—brick-and-mortar or virtual—you'll pay a fee for the service. And know that the service you get from some online agents isn't comprehensive. For example Expedia and Travelocity don't search for prices on budget airlines like jetBlue, Southwest, or small foreign carriers. That said, some agents (online or not) *do* have access to fares that are difficult to find otherwise, and the savings can more than make up for any surcharge.

A knowledgeable brick-and-mortar travel agent can be a godsend if you're booking a cruise, a package trip that's not available to you directly, an air pass, or a complicated itinerary including several overseas flights. What's more, travel agents that specialize in a destination may have exclusive access to certain deals and insider information on things such as charter flights. Agents who specialize in types of travelers (senior citizens, gays and lesbians, naturists) or types of trips (cruises, luxury travel, safaris) can also be invaluable.

■TIP→Remember that Expedia, Travelocity, and Orbitz are travel agents, not just booking engines. To resolve any problems with a reservation made through these companies, contact them first.

A top-notch agent planning your trip to Russia will make sure you get the correct visa application and complete it on time; the one booking your cruise may get you a cabin upgrade or arrange to have bottle of champagne chilling in your cabin when you embark. And complain about the surcharges all you like, but when things don't work out the way you'd hoped, it's nice to have an agent to put things right.

Agent Resources **American Society of Travel Agents** (☎703/739–2782 ⊕www.travelsense.org).

▌ ACCOMMODATIONS

Most hotels and other lodgings require you to give your credit-card details before they will confirm your reservation. If you don't feel comfortable e-mailing this information, ask if you can fax it (some places even prefer faxes). However you book, get confirmation in writing and have a copy of it handy when you check in.

Be sure you understand the hotel's cancellation policy. Some places allow you to cancel without any kind of penalty—even if you prepaid to secure a discounted rate—if you cancel at least 24 hours in advance. Others require you to cancel

Online Booking Resources

AGGREGATORS		
Kayak	www.kayak.com;	also looks at cruises and vacation packages.
Mobissimo	www.mobissimo.com	
Qixo	www.qixo.com	also compares cruises, vacation packages, and even travel insurance.
Sidestep	www.sidestep.com	also compares vacation packages and lists travel deals.
Travelgrove	www.travelgrove.com	also compares cruises and packages.
Booking Engines		
Cheap Tickets	www.cheaptickets.com	a discounter.
Expedia	www.expedia.com	a large online agency that charges a booking fee for airline tickets.
Hotwire	www.hotwire.com	a discounter.
lastminute.com	www.lastminute.com	specializes in last-minute travel the main site is for the U.K., but it has a link to a U.S. site.
Onetravel.com	www.onetravel.com	a discounter for hotels, car rentals, airfares, and packages.
Orbitz	www.orbitz.com	charges a booking fee for airline tickets, but gives a clear breakdown of fees and taxes before you book.
Travel.com	www.travel.com	allows you to compare its rates with those of other booking engines.
Travelocity	www.travelocity.com	charges a booking fee for airline tickets, but promises good problem resolution.
ONLINE ACCOMMODATIONS		
Hotelbook.com	www.hotelbook.com	focuses on independent hotels worldwide.
Hotel Club	www.hotelclub.net	good for major cities worldwide.
Hotels.com	www.hotels.com	a big Expedia-owned wholesaler that offers rooms in hotels all over the world.

a week in advance or penalize you the cost of one night. Small inns and B&Bs are most likely to require you to cancel far in advance. Most hotels allow children under a certain age to stay in their parents' room at no extra charge, but others charge for them as extra adults; find out the cutoff age for discounts.

■TIP→ Assume that hotels operate on the European Plan (**EP**, no meals) unless we specify that they use the Breakfast Plan (**BP**, with full breakfast), Continental Plan (**CP**, Continental breakfast), Full American Plan (**FAP**, all meals), Modified American Plan (**MAP**, breakfast and dinner) or are **all-inclusive** (**AI**, all meals and most activities).

APARTMENT & HOUSE RENTALS

ONLINE BOOKING RESOURCES

Contacts At Home Abroad (☎212/421–9165 ⊕www.athome abroadinc.com). **Barclay International Group** (☎516/364–0064 or 800/845–6636 ⊕www.barclayweb. com). **Vacation Home Rentals Worldwide** (☎201/767–9393 or 800/633–3284 ⊕www.vhrww. com). **Villanet** (☎206/417–3444 or 800/964–1891 ⊕www.rentavilla. com). **Villas & Apartments Abroad** (☎212/213–6435 or 800/433–3020 ⊕www.vaanyc.com). **Villas International** (☎415/499–9490 or 800/221–2260 ⊕www.villas intl.com). **Villas of Distinction** (☎707/778–1800 or 800/289–0900 ⊕www.villasofdistinction.com). **Wimco** (☎800/449–1553 ⊕www.wimco.com).

HOME EXCHANGES

With a direct home exchange you stay in someone else's home while they stay in yours. Some outfits also deal with vacation homes, so you're not actually staying in someone's full-time residence, just their vacant weekend place.

Exchange Clubs Home Exchange. com (☎800/877–8723 ⊕www. homeexchange.com); $59.95 for a 1-year online listing. **HomeLink International** (☎800/638–3841 ⊕www.homelink.org); $90 yearly for Web-only membership; $140 includes Web access and two catalogs. **Intervac U.S.** (☎800/756–4663 ⊕www.intervacus.com); $78.88 for Web-only membership; $126 includes Web access and a catalog.

❚ AIRLINE TICKETS

Most domestic airline tickets are electronic; international tickets may be either electronic or paper. With an e-ticket the only thing you receive is an e-mailed receipt citing your itinerary and reservation and ticket numbers.

The greatest advantage of an e-ticket is that if you lose your receipt, you can simply print out another copy or ask the airline to do it for you at check-in. You usually pay a surcharge (up to $50) to get a paper ticket, if you can get one at all.

The sole advantage of a paper ticket is that it may be easier to endorse over to another airline if your flight is canceled and the airline with which you booked

1. Join "frequent guest" programs. You may get preferential treatment in room choice and/or upgrades.

2. Call direct. You can sometimes get a better price if you call a hotel's local toll-free number (if available) rather than a central reservations number.

3. Check online. Check hotel Web sites, as not all chains are represented on all travel sites.

4. Look for price guarantees. For overseas trips, look for guaranteed rates. With your rate locked in you won't pay more, even if the price goes up in the local currency.

5. Look for weekend deals at business hotels. High-end chains catering to business travelers are often busy only on weekdays; to fill rooms they often drop rates dramatically on weekends.

6. Know when to go. Avoid peak-season travel when possible. If your dates straddle peak and nonpeak seasons, a property may still charge peak-season rates for the entire stay.

7. Weigh your options (we can't say this enough). Weigh transportation times and costs against the savings of staying in a hotel that's cheaper because it's out of the way.

can't accommodate you on another flight.

■TIP→ Discount air passes that let you travel economically in a country or region must often be purchased before you leave home. In some cases you can only get them through a travel agent.

RENTAL CARS

When you reserve a car, ask about cancellation penalties, taxes, drop-off charges (if you're planning to pick up the car in one city and leave it in another), and surcharges (for being under or over a certain age, for additional drivers, or for driving across state or country borders or beyond a specific distance from your point of rental). All these things can add substantially to your costs. Request car seats and extras such as GPS when you book.

Rates are sometimes—but not always—better if you book in advance or reserve through a rental agency's Web site. There are other reasons to book ahead, though: for popular destinations, during busy times of the year, or to ensure that you get certain types of cars (vans, SUVs, exotic sports cars).

■TIP→ Make sure that a confirmed reservation guarantees you a car. Agencies sometimes overbook, particularly for busy weekends and holiday periods.

Taxi fares are steep, and a car can come in handy if you plan to dine at the Corridor hotels or travel frequently between the two towns, or if you're spending more than a few days in Los Cabos. If you don't want to rent a car, your hotel concierge or tour operator can arrange for a car with a driver or limousine service.

Convertibles and jeeps are popular rentals, but beware of sunburn and windburn and remember there's nowhere to stash your belongings out of sight. Specify whether you want air-conditioning and manual or automatic transmission. If you rent from a major U.S.-based company, you can find a car for about $40 per day ($280 per week), including automatic transmission, unlimited mileage, and 10% tax; insurance will add $19 to $25 per day, depending on the company, so you should figure the cost of insurance into your budget. You will pay considerably more (probably double) for a higher-end car with air-conditioning. Most vendors negotiate considerably if tourism is slow; ask about special rates if you're renting by the week.

To increase the likelihood of getting the car you want, make arrangements before you leave for your trip. Also, call around, because rates can vary widely. You can sometimes, but not always, find cheaper rates on the Internet, but no matter how you book, rates are generally much lower when you reserve a car in advance outside of Mexico.

In Mexico your own driver's license is acceptable. In most cases, the minimum rental age is 25, although some companies will lower it to 22 for an extra daily charge. A valid driver's license, major credit card, and Mexican car insurance are required.

CAR RENTAL RESOURCES

Automobile Associations U.S.: **American Automobile Association** (AAA ☎315/797-5000 ⊕www. aaa.com); most contact with the organization is through state and regional members. **National Automobile Club** (☎650/294-7000 ⊕www.thenac.com); membership is open to California residents only.

Major Agencies Alamo (☎800/522-9696 ⊕www.alamo. com). **Avis** (☎800/331-1084 ⊕www.avis.com). **Budget** (☎800/472-3325 ⊕www.budget. com). **Hertz** (☎800/654-3001 ⊕www.hertz.com). **National Car Rental** (☎800/227-7368 ⊕www. nationalcar.com).

CAR-RENTAL INSURANCE

Everyone who rents a car wonders whether the insurance that the rental companies offer is worth the expense. No one—including us—has a simple answer. It all depends on how much regular insurance you have, how comfortable you are with risk, and whether or not money is an issue.

If you own a car, your personal auto insurance may cover a rental to some degree, though not all policies protect you abroad; always read your policy's fine print. If you don't have auto insurance, then seriously consider buying the collision- or loss-damage waiver (CDW or LDW) from the car-rental company, which eliminates your liability for damage to the car. Some credit cards offer CDW coverage, but it's usually supplemental to your own insurance and rarely covers SUVs, minivans, luxury models, and the like. If your coverage is secondary, you may still be liable for loss-of-use costs from the car-rental company. But no credit-card insurance is valid unless you use that card for *all* transactions, from reserving to paying the final bill. All companies exclude car rental in some countries, so be sure to find out about the destination to which you are traveling.

■TIP→ Diners Club offers primary CDW coverage on all rentals reserved and paid for with the card. This means that Diners Club's company—not your own car insurance—pays in case of an accident. It *doesn't* mean your car-insurance company won't raise your rates once it discovers you had an accident.

Some rental agencies require you to purchase CDW coverage; many will even include it in quoted rates. All will strongly encourage you to buy CDW—possibly implying that it's required—so be sure to ask about such things before renting. In most cases it's cheaper to add a supplemental CDW plan to your comprehensive travel-insurance policy (⇨ *Trip Insurance under Things to Consider in Getting Started, above*) than to purchase it from a rental company. That said, you don't want to pay for a supplement if you're required to buy insurance from the rental company.

You must **carry Mexican auto insurance.** If you injure anyone in an accident, you could well be jailed—whether it was your fault or not—unless you have insurance. It is difficult to arrange bail once you are jailed, and it can take months for your case to be heard by the courts. If you're an AAA (American Automobile Association) member, you can purchase Mexican insurance in advance; call your local AAA office for details.

■TIP→ You can decline the insurance from the rental company and purchase it through a third-party provider such as Travel Guard (⊕www.travelguard.com)—$9 per day for $35,000 of coverage. That's sometimes just under half the price of the CDW offered by some car-rental companies.

▌VACATION PACKAGES

Packages *are not* guided excursions. Packages combine airfare, accommodations, and perhaps a rental car or other extras (theater tickets, guided excursions, boat trips, reserved entry to popular museums, transit passes), but they let you do your own thing. During busy periods packages may be your only option, as flights and rooms may be sold out otherwise.

Packages will definitely save you time. They can also save you money, particularly in peak seasons, but—and this is a really big "but"—you should price each part of the package separately to be sure. And be aware that prices advertised on Web sites and in newspapers rarely include service charges or taxes, which can up your costs by hundreds of dollars.

■TIP→ Some packages and cruises are sold only through travel agents. Don't always assume that you can get the best deal by booking everything yourself.

Each year consumers are stranded or lose their money when packagers—even large ones with excellent reputations—go out of business. How can you protect yourself?

First, always pay with a credit card; if you have a problem, your credit-card company may help you resolve it. Second, buy trip

8 WAYS TO SAVE

1. Nonrefundable is best. Just remember that you'll pay dearly if you change your plans.

2. Comparison shop. Web sites and travel agents can have different arrangements with the airlines and offer different prices for exactly the same flights.

3. Watch those ticketing fees. Surcharges are usually added when you buy your ticket anywhere but on an airline Web site.

4. Check often. Start looking for cheap fares from three months out to about one month. Keep looking till you find a price you like.

5. Don't work alone. Some Web sites have tracking features that will e-mail you immediately when good deals are posted.

6. Jump on the good deals. Waiting even a few minutes might mean paying more.

7. Be flexible. Look for departures on Tuesday, Wednesday, and Saturday, typically the cheapest days to travel. And check on prices for departures at different times and to and from alternative airports.

8. Weigh your options. What you get can be as important as what you save. A cheaper flight might have a long layover, or it might land at a secondary airport, where your ground transportation costs might be higher.

7 WAYS TO SAVE

1. Rent weekly. Weekly rates are usually better than daily ones. Even if you only want to rent for five or six days, ask for the weekly rate; it may very well be cheaper than the daily rate for that period of time.

2. Don't forget the locals. Price local companies as well as the majors.

3. Airport rentals can cost more. Airports often add surcharges, which you can sometimes avoid by renting from an agency whose office is just off airport property.

4. Wholesalers can help. Investigate wholesalers, which don't own fleets but rent in bulk from firms that do, and which frequently offer better rates.

5. Pump it yourself. Don't prepay for rental car gas. The savings isn't that great, and unless you coast in on empty upon return, you wind up paying for gas you don't use.

6. Get all your discounts. Find out whether a credit card you carry or organization or frequent-renter program to which you belong has a discount program. But confirm that such discounts really are a deal.

7. Check out packages. Adding a car rental onto your air/hotel vacation package may be cheaper than renting a car separately.

insurance that covers default. Third, choose a company that belongs to the United States Tour Operators Association, whose members must set aside funds to cover defaults. Finally, choose a company that also participates in the Tour Operator Program of the American Society of Travel Agents (ASTA), which will act as mediator in any disputes.

You can also check on the tour operator's reputation among travelers by posting an inquiry on one of the Fodors.com forums.

Organizations American Society of Travel Agents (ASTA ☎703/739–2782 or 800/965–2782 ⊕www.astanet.com). **United States Tour Operators Association** (USTOA ☎212/599–6599 ⊕www. ustoa.com).

■ TIP→ Local tourism boards can provide information about lesser-known and small-niche operators that sell packages to only a few destinations.

TRANSPORTATION

BY AIR

You can now fly nonstop to Los
Cabos from Southern Califor-
nia, Texas, or Arizona. From
most other destinations, you will
have to make a connecting flight,
either in the U.S. or in Mexico
City. Via nonstop service, Los
Cabos is about 2 hours from
San Diego, about 2¼ hours from
Houston, 3 hours from Dal-
las/Fort Worth, 2½ hours from
Los Angeles, and 2½ hours from
Phoenix. Flying time from New
York to Mexico City, where you
must switch planes to continue
to Los Cabos, is 5 hours. Los
Cabos is about a 2 ½-hour flight
from Mexico City.

Airlines & Airports Airline and
Airport Links.com (⊕www.airlin-
eandairportlinks.com) has links
to many of the world's airlines
and airports.

Airline Security Issues Transportation Security Administration
(⊕www.tsa.gov) has answers for
almost every question that might
come up.

AIRPORTS
Aeropuerto Internacional Los
Cabos is 1 km (½ mi) west of the
Transpeninsular Highway (Hwy.
1), 13 km (8 mi) north of San
José del Cabo, and 48 km (30 mi)
northeast of Cabo San Lucas. The
airport has restaurants, duty-free
shops, and car-rental agencies.
Alaska Airlines has a separate terminal with all services at the airport. Los Cabos flights increase in
winter with seasonal flights from
U.S. airlines.

Aeropuerto General Manuel
Márquez de León serves La Paz.
It's 11 km (7 mi) northwest of
the Baja California Sur capital,
which itself is 188 km (117 mi)
northwest of Los Cabos.

Airport Information Aeropuerto
General Manuel Márquez de
León (☎612/112–0082). Aeropuerto Internacional Los Cabos
(☎624/146–5013).

GROUND TRANSPORTATION
If you have purchased a vacation package from an airline or
travel agency, transfers are usually included. Otherwise, only
the most exclusive hotels in Los
Cabos offer transfers. Fares from
the airport to hotels in Los Cabos
are expensive. The least expensive transport is by shuttle buses
that stop at various hotels along
the route; fares run $12 to $25
per person. Private taxi fares run
from $20 to $40. Some hotels
can arrange a pickup, which
is much faster and might cost
about the same as a shuttle. Ask
about hotel transfers if you're
staying in the East Cape, La Paz,
and Todos Santos, and you're
not renting a car—cab fares to
these areas are astronomical.

Unless you want to tour a time-share or real estate property, ignore the offers for free transfers when you come out of customs. The scene can be bewildering for first timers. Sales representatives from various time-share properties compete vociferously for clients; often you won't realize you've been suckered into a time-share presentation until you get in the van. To avoid this situation, go to the official taxi booths inside the baggage claim or just outside the final customs clearance area and pay for a ticket for a regular shuttle bus. Private taxis, often U.S. vans, are expensive and not metered, so always ask the fare before getting in. Rates change frequently, but for one to four persons, it costs about $15 to get to San José del Cabo, $26 to a hotel along the Corridor, and $50 to Cabo San Lucas. After the fourth passenger, it's about an additional $3 per person. Usually only vans accept more than four passengers. At the end of your trip, don't wait until the last minute to book return transport. Make arrangements a few days in advance for shuttle service, or sign up at your hotel to share a cab with other travelers.

FLIGHTS

AeroCalafia flies charter flights from Los Cabos for whale-watching. AeroCalifornia flies nonstop to Los Cabos from Los Angeles. It also serves La Paz from Tijuana, Tucson, and Los Angeles, and has daily flights from Los Angeles to Loreto.

Aeroméxico has service to Los Cabos from San Diego, to Loreto from San Diego, Los Angeles, Hermosillo, and Mexico City, and to La Paz from Los Angeles, Tucson, Tijuana, and Mexico City.

Alaska Airlines flies nonstop to Los Cabos from Los Angeles, San Diego, Seattle, Portland, and San Francisco, twice weekly to Loreto from Los Angeles, and three times a week to La Paz from Los Angeles. America West has nonstop service from Phoenix. American flies nonstop from Dallas/Fort Worth, Chicago, and Los Angeles. British Airways and other European airlines fly to Mexico City, where connections are made for the two-hour flight to Los Cabos.

Continental has nonstop service from Houston. Delta flies to Los Cabos from Atlanta and Ontario, CA, and has daily flights from Los Angeles to La Paz. Mexicana offers flights from Sacramento, Los Angeles, and Denver.

Airline Contacts AeroCalafia (☎624/143–4302 in Los Cabos). **AeroCalifornia** (☎612/123–9800 in La Paz, 624/143–3700 in Los Cabos, 800/237–6225 in U.S. ⊕www.aerocalifornia.com). **Aeroméxico** (☎624/146–5097 in Los Cabos, 612/124–6366 in La Paz, 613/135–1837 in Loreto, 800/237–6639 in U.S. ⊕www.aeromexico.com). **Alaska Airlines** (☎800/426–0333, 624/146–5101 in Los Cabos ⊕www.alaskaair.com). **American Airlines** (☎800/433–7300, 624/146–5303 in Los Cabos ⊕www.

FLYING 101

Flying may not be as carefree as it once was, but there are some things you can do to make your trip smoother.

Minimize the time spent standing line. Buy an e-ticket, check in at an electronic kiosk, or—even better—check in on your airline's Web site before leaving home.

Arrive when you need to. Research your airline's policy. It's usually at least an hour before domestic flights and two to three hours before international flights. But airlines at some busy airports have more stringent requirements.

Get to the gate. If you aren't at the gate at least 10 minutes before your flight is scheduled to take off (sometimes earlier), you won't be allowed to board.

Double-check your flight times. Do this especially if you reserved far in advance. Schedules change, and alerts may not reach you.

Don't go hungry. Ask whether your airline offers anything to eat; even when it does, be prepared to pay.

Get the seat you want. Often, you can pick a seat when you buy your ticket on an airline Web site. You can also select a seat if you check in electronically.

Check your scheduling. Don't buy a ticket if there's less than an hour between connecting flights. Although schedules are padded, if anything goes wrong you might miss your connection. If you're traveling to an important function, depart a day early.

Bring paper. Even when using an e-ticket, always carry a hard copy of your receipt; you may need it to get your boarding pass, which most airports require to get past security.

Complain at the airport. If your baggage goes astray or your flight goes awry, complain before leaving the airport. Most carriers require this.

Beware of overbooked flights. If a flight is oversold, the gate agent will usually ask for volunteers and offer some sort of compensation for taking a different flight. If you're bumped from a flight *involuntarily*, the airline must give you some kind of compensation if an alternate flight can't be found within one hour.

Know your rights. If your flight is delayed because of something within the airline's control (bad weather doesn't count), the airline must get you to your destination on the same day, even if they have to book you on another airline and in an upgraded class. Read the Contract of Carriage, which is usually buried on the airline's Web site.

Be prepared. The Boy Scout motto is especially important if you're traveling during a stormy season. To quickly adjust your plans, program a few numbers into your cell: your airline, an airport hotel or two, your destination hotel, your car service, and/or your travel agent.

aa.com). **Continental Airlines**
(☎800/523–3273, 624/146–5040 in
Los Cabos ⊕www.continental.com).
Delta Airlines (☎800/241–4141,
624/146–5005 in Los Cabos ⊕www.
delta.com). **Mexicana** (☎800/531–
7921, 624/146–5001 in Los Cabos
⊕www.mexicana.com). **USAirways**
(☎800/235–9292, 624/146–5380 in
Los Cabos ⊕www.usairways.com).

▌ BY BUS

In Los Cabos, the main Terminal de Autobus (Los Cabos Bus
Terminal) is about a 10-minute
drive west of Cabo San Lucas.
Express buses with air-conditioning and restrooms travel
frequently from the terminal to
Todos Santos (one hour) and La
Paz (three hours). One-way fare
is $4 (payable in pesos or dol-
lars) to Todos Santos, $14 to La
Paz. From the Corridor, expect
to pay about $25 for a taxi to
the bus station.

SuburBaja can provide private
transport for $60 between San
José del Cabo and Cabo San
Lucas.

In La Paz the main Terminal de
Autobus is 10 blocks from the
malecón. Bus companies offer
service to Los Cabos (three
hours), Loreto (five hours),
and Guerrero Negro (the buses
stop at the highway entrance to
town). The Guerrero Negro trip
takes anywhere from six to nine
hours, and buses stop in Santa
Rosalia and San Ignacio.

Bus Information **Los Cabos
Terminal de Autobus** (✉Hwy. 19

☎624/143–5020 or 624/143–7880).
SuburBaja (☎624/146–0888).

▌ BY CAR

Rental cars come in handy
when exploring Baja. Countless paved and dirt roads branch
off Highway 1 like octopus ten-
tacles beckoning adventurers
toward the mountains, ocean,
and sea. Baja Sur's highways and
city streets are under constant
improvement, and Highway 1 is
usually in good condition except
during heavy rains. Four-wheel
drive comes in handy for hard-
core backcountry explorations,
but isn't necessary most of the
time. Just be aware that some
car-rental companies void their
insurance policies if you run into
trouble off paved roads.

GASOLINE

Pemex (the government petro-
leum monopoly) franchises all
gas stations in Mexico. Stations
are on the outskirts of San José
del Cabo and Cabo San Lucas
and in the Corridor. Gas is mea-
sured in liters. Gas stations in
Los Cabos may not accept credit cards. Prices run higher than
in the United States. Premium
unleaded gas (*magna premio*)
and regular unleaded gas (*magna sin*) is available nationwide,
but it's still a good idea to fill up
whenever you can. Fuel quality is
generally lower than that in the
United States and Europe. Vehicles with fuel-injected engines
are likely to have problems after
driving extended distances.

Gas-station attendants pump the gas for you and may also wash your windshield and check your oil and tire air pressure. A tip of 5 or 10 pesos (about 50¢ or $1) is customary depending on the number of services rendered, beyond pumping gas.

ROAD CONDITIONS

Mexico Highway 1, also known as the Carretera Transpeninsular, runs the entire 1,700 km (1,054 mi) from Tijuana to Cabo San Lucas. Occasional bad weather and repairs can make for slow going. Do not drive the highway at high speeds or at night—it is not lighted.

Highway 19 runs between Cabo San Lucas and Todos Santos, joining Highway 1 below La Paz. The four-lane road between San José del Cabo and Cabo San Lucas is usually in good condition, although dips and bridges become flooded in heavy rains and sections are frequently destroyed by hurricanes. Roadwork along the highway is common.

In rural areas, roads are quite poor. Use caution, especially during the rainy season, when rock slides and potholes are a problem, and be alert for animals—cattle, coyotes, and dogs in particular—especially on the highways. If you have a long distance to cover, start early and fill up on gas; don't let your tank get below half full. Allow extra time for unforeseen obstacles.

Signage is not always adequate in Mexico, and the best advice is to travel with a companion and a good map. Always lock your car, and never leave valuable items in the body of the car (the trunk will suffice for daytime outings, but don't pack it in front of prying eyes).

The Mexican Tourism Ministry distributes free road maps from its tourism offices outside the country. Guía Roji and Pemex publish current city, regional, and national road maps, which are available in bookstores and big supermarket chains for under $10; gas stations generally do not carry maps.

ROADSIDE EMERGENCIES

The Mexican Tourism Ministry operates a fleet of more than 350 pickup trucks, known as the Angeles Verdes, or Green Angels. Bilingual drivers provide mechanical help, first aid, radio-telephone communication, basic supplies and small parts, towing, tourist information, and protection. Services are free; spare parts, fuel, and lubricants are provided at cost. Tips are always appreciated ($5–$10 for big jobs, $2–$3 for minor repairs). The Green Angels patrol sections of the major highways daily 8–8 (later on holiday weekends). If you break down, **pull off the road as far as possible,** lift the hood of your car, hail a passing vehicle, and ask the driver to **notify the patrol.** Most bus and truck drivers will be quite helpful. If you witness an accident, do not stop to help—it could be a ploy to rob you or could get you interminably involved with the police. Instead, notify the nearest official.

Contacts **Green Angels, La Paz** (☎612/125–9677).

SAFETY ON THE ROAD

The mythical *banditos* are not a big concern in Baja. Still, **never drive at night,** especially in rural areas. Cows and burros grazing alongside the road can pose a real danger—you never know when they'll decide to wander into traffic. Other good reasons for not driving at night include potholes, cars with no working lights, road-hogging trucks, and difficulty with getting assistance. Plan driving times, and if night is falling, find a nearby hotel.

Though it isn't common in Los Cabos, police may pull you over for supposedly breaking the law, or for being a good prospect for a scam. If it happens to you, remember to **be polite**—displays of anger will only make matters worse—and be aware that a police officer might be pulling you over for something you didn't do. Corruption is a fact of life in Mexico, and the $5 it costs to get your license back is definitely supplementary income for the officer who pulled you over with no intention of taking you to police headquarters.

If you're stopped for speeding, the officer is supposed to hold your license until you pay the fine at the local police station. But he will always prefer taking a *mordida* (small bribe) to wasting his time at the police station. If you decide to dispute a preposterous charge, do so with a smile, and tell the officer that you would like to talk to the police captain when you get to the station. The officer usually will let you go.

▎ BY TAXI

Taxis are plentiful throughout Baja Sur, even in the smallest towns. Government-certified taxis have a license with a photo of the driver and a taxi number prominently displayed. Fares are exorbitant in Los Cabos, and the taxi union is very powerful. Some visitors have taken to boycotting taxis completely, using rental cars and buses instead. The fare between Cabo San Lucas and San José del Cabo runs about $45—more at night. Cabs from Corridor hotels to either town run about $25 each way. Expect to pay at least $30 from the airport to hotels in San José, and closer to $65 to San Lucas.

In La Paz, taxis are readily available and inexpensive. A ride within town costs under $5; a trip to Pichilingue costs between $7 and $10. Illegitimate taxis aren't a problem in this region.

ON THE GROUND

ADDRESSES

Many addresses in Mexico have "s/n" for *sin número* (no number) after the street name. This is common throughout Mexico, as is the practice of listing cross streets in an address. Similarly, many Cabo hotels give their address as "Carretera Cabo San Lucas–San José del Cabo, Km 19," which indicates that the property is at the 19th kilometer on the *carretera* (main highway) between Cabo San Lucas and San José del Cabo. Some properties in the Corridor call the highway the "Corredor Turistico" or the "Carretera Transpeninsular," although this book refers to this road as Highway 1.

Other abbreviations used in addresses include the following: Av. (*avenida*, or avenue), Calz. (*calzada*, or road), Fracc. (*fraccionamiento*, or housing estate), and Int. (*interior*).

Addresses in Mexico are written with the street name first, followed by the street number. A five-digit *código postal* (C.P.; postal code) precedes, rather than follows, the name of the city. Apdo. (*apartado*) is short for box; Apdo. Postal, or A.P., means post-office box number.

▌ COMMUNICATIONS

INTERNET

Cabo Mail Internet in Cabo San Lucas has several computers and charges $10 an hour. Trazzo Digital in San José del Cabo offers access for $10 an hour. Galería Don Tomás in La Paz has Internet access in artful surroundings. Baja Net in La Paz has ports for laptops along with many computer terminals. Both places charge about $10 an hour.

Contacts **Baja Net** (⊠Av. Madero 430, La Paz ☎612/125-9380). **Cabo Mail Internet** (⊠Blvd. Cárdenas, Cabo San Lucas ☎624/143-7797). **Cybercafes** (⊕www.cybercafes.com) lists more than 4,000 Internet cafés worldwide. **Trazzo Digital** (⊠Calle Zaragoza 24, San José del Cabo ☎624/142-0303).

PHONES

The good news is that you can now make a direct-dial telephone call from virtually any point on earth. The bad news? You can't always do so cheaply. Calling from a hotel is almost always the most expensive option; hotels usually add huge surcharges to all calls, particularly international ones. In some countries you can phone from call centers or even the post office. Calling cards usually keep costs to a minimum, but only if you purchase them locally. And then there are mobile phones (⇨*below*), which are sometimes more prevalent—

particularly in the developing world—than land lines; as expensive as mobile phone calls can be, they are still usually a much cheaper option than calling from your hotel.

Los Cabos has good telephone service, with pay phone booths along the streets and the Corridor. Most phones have Touch-Tone (digital) circuitry. Phone numbers in Mexico change frequently; a recording may offer the new number, so it's useful to learn the Spanish words for numbers 1 through 9. Beware of pay phones and hotel-room phones with signs saying "Call Home" and other enticements. Some of these phone companies charge astronomical rates.

The country code for Mexico is 52. When calling a Mexico number from abroad, dial the country code and then the area code and local number. At this writing, the area code for all of Los Cabos is 624. All local numbers now have seven digits.

CALLING WITHIN MEXICO

For local or long-distance calls, one option is to find a *caseta de larga distancia*, a telephone service usually operated out of a small business; look for the phone symbol on the door. Casetas have become less common as pay phones have begun to appear even in the smallest towns. Rates at casetas seem to vary widely, so shop around. Sometimes you can make collect calls from casetas, and sometimes you cannot, depending on the operator

CON OR CONCIERGE?

Good hotel concierges can be invaluable—for arranging transportation, getting reservations at the hottest restaurant, and scoring tickets for a sold-out show or entree to an exclusive nightclub.

However, it's not uncommon for restaurants to ply concierges with free food and drink in exchange for steering diners their way. Indeed, European concierges often receive referral *fees*. Hotel chains usually have guidelines about what their concierges can accept. The best concierges, however, are above reproach. This is particularly true of those who belong to the prestigious international society of Les Clefs d'Or.

What can you expect of a concierge? At a typical tourist-class hotel you can expect him or her to give you the basics: to show you something on a map, make a standard restaurant reservation (particularly if you don't speak the language), or help you book a tour or airport transportation. In Asia concierges perform the vital service of writing out the name or address of your destination for you to give to a cab driver.

Savvy concierges at the finest hotels and resorts, can arrange for just about any good or service imaginable—and do so quickly. You should compensate them appropriately. A $10 tip is enough to show appreciation for a table at a hot restaurant. But the reward should be greater for any of those hard-to-get-tickets.

and possibly your degree of visible desperation. Casetas generally charge 50¢–$1.50 to place a collect call (some charge by the minute); it's usually better to call *por cobrar* (collect) from a pay phone.

CALLING OUTSIDE MEXICO
To make a call to the United States or Canada, dial 001 before the area code and number. For operator assistance in making an international call dial 090.

AT&T, MCI, and Sprint access codes make calling long-distance relatively convenient, but you may find the local access number blocked in many hotel rooms. First ask the hotel operator to connect you. If the hotel operator balks, ask for an international operator, or dial the international operator yourself. One way to improve your odds of getting connected to your long-distance carrier is to travel with more than one company's calling card (a hotel may block Sprint, for example, but not MCI). If all else fails, call from a pay phone.

Access Codes **AT&T Direct** (☎01–800/462-4240). **MCI World-Phone** (☎01–800/674-7000). **Sprint International Access** (☎01–800/877-8000).

DIRECTORY & OPERATOR ASSISTANCE
Directory assistance in Mexico is 040 nationwide. For international assistance, dial 020 first for an international operator and most likely you'll get one who speaks English; indicate in which city, state, and country you require directory assistance and you will be connected with directory assistance there.

MOBILE PHONES
If you have a multiband phone (some countries use different frequencies than what's used in the United States) and your service provider uses the world-standard GSM network (as do T-Mobile, Cingular, and Verizon), you can probably use your phone abroad. Roaming fees can be steep, however: 99¢ a minute is considered reasonable. And overseas you normally pay the toll charges for incoming calls. It's almost always cheaper to send a text message than to make a call, since text messages have a very low set fee (often less than 5¢).

If you just want to make local calls, consider buying a new SIM card (note that your provider may have to unlock your phone for you to use a different SIM card) and a prepaid service plan in the destination. You'll then have a local number and can make local calls at local rates. If your trip is extensive, you could also simply buy a new cell phone in your destination, as the initial cost will be offset over time.

■TIP➜**If you travel internationally frequently, save one of your old mobile phones or buy a cheap one on the Internet; ask your cell phone company to unlock it for you, and take it with you as a travel phone, buying a new SIM card**

GETTING STARTED / BOOKING YOUR TRIP / TRANSPORTATION / ON THE GROUND with pay-as-you-go service in each destination.

Contacts **Cellular Abroad** (☎800/287–5072 ⊕www.cellular-abroad.com) rents and sells GMS phones and sells SIM cards that work in many countries. **Mobal** (☎888/888–9162 ⊕www.mobalrental.com) rents mobiles and sells GSM phones (starting at $49) that will operate in 140 countries. Per-call rates vary throughout the world. **Planet Fone** (☎888/988–4777 ⊕www.planetfone.com) rents cell phones, but the per-minute rates are expensive.

PUBLIC PHONES

Occasionally you'll see traditional black, square pay phones with push buttons or dials; although they have a coin slot on top, local calls are free. However, these coin-only pay phones are usually broken. Newer pay phones have an unmarked slot for prepaid phone cards called Telmex cards. The cards are sold in 30-, 50-, or 100-peso denominations at newsstands or pharmacies. Credit is deleted from the Telmex card as you use it, and your balance is displayed on a small screen on the phone. Some phones have two unmarked slots, one for a Telmex card and the other for a credit card. These are primarily for Mexican bank cards, but some accept Visa or MasterCard.

TOLL-FREE NUMBERS

Toll-free numbers in Mexico start with an 800 prefix. To reach them, you need to dial 01 before the number. In this guide, Mexico-only toll-free numbers appear as follows: 01–800/123–4567 (numbers have seven digits). Most of the 800 numbers in this book work in the U.S. only and are listed simply: 800/123–4567; you cannot access a U.S. 800 number from Mexico. Some U.S. toll-free numbers ring directly at Mexican properties. Don't be deterred if someone answers the phone in Spanish. Simply ask for someone who speaks English. Toll-free numbers that work in other countries are labeled accordingly.

❚ CUSTOMS & DUTIES

You're always allowed to bring goods of a certain value back home without having to pay any duty or import tax. But there's a limit on the amount of tobacco and liquor you can bring back duty-free, and some countries have separate limits for perfumes; for exact figures, check with your customs department. The values of so-called "duty-free" goods are included in these amounts. When you shop abroad, save all your receipts, as customs inspectors may ask to see them as well as the items you purchased. If the total value of your goods is more than the duty-free limit, you'll have to pay a tax (most often a flat percentage) on the value of everything beyond that limit.

You aren't allowed to bring meat, vegetables, plants, fruit, or flowers into the country, so don't consider bringing your own food if you're renting a villa.

Mexican Customs (Aduana Mexico) has a very thorough Web site, but everything is in Spanish.

Information in Mexico **Aduana Mexico** (⊕www.aduanas.sat.gob.mx).

U.S. Information **U.S. Customs and Border Protection** (⊕www.cbp.gov).

▌ ELECTRICITY

For U.S. and Canadian travelers, electrical converters are not necessary because Mexico operates on the 60-cycle, 120-volt system; however, many Mexican outlets have not been updated to accommodate three-prong and polarized plugs (those with one larger prong), so to be safe bring an adapter. If your appliances are dual-voltage you'll need only an adapter. Don't use 110-volt outlets, marked FOR SHAVERS ONLY, for high-wattage appliances such as blow dryers. Most laptops operate equally well on 110 and 220 volts and so require only an adapter.

Contacts **Steve Kropla's Help for World Traveler's** (⊕www.kropla. com) has information on electrical and telephone plugs around the world. **Walkabout Travel Gear** (⊕www.walkabouttravelgear.com) has a good coverage of electricity under "adapters."

▌ EMERGENCIES

The state of Baja California Sur has instituted an emergency number for police and fire: 060. A second number, 065, is available to summon medical assistance. Both numbers can be used throughout the state, and there are English-speaking operators. For medical emergencies, Tourist Medical Assist has English-speaking physicians who make emergency calls around the clock.

Emergency Services **Highway Patrol** (☎624/146–0573 in San José del Cabo, 612/122–0369 in La Paz). **Police** (☎624/142–2835 in San José del Cabo, 624/143–3977 in Cabo San Lucas, 612/122–0477 in La Paz).

FOREIGN EMBASSIES
Hospitals & Clinics **AmeriMed** (✉Blvd. Cárdenas at Paseo Marina, Cabo San Lucas ☎624/143–9670). **Centro de Especialidades Médicas** (✉Calle Delfines 110, La Paz ☎612/124–0400).

Pharmacies **AmeriMed** (✉Blvd. Cárdenas at Paseo Marina, Cabo San Lucas ☎624/143–9670). **Farmacia Baja California** (✉Calle Independencia at Calle Madero, La Paz ☎612/122–0240).

▌ HEALTH

The most common types of illnesses are caused by contaminated food and water. Especially in developing countries, drink only bottled, boiled, or purified water and drinks; don't drink from public fountains or use ice. You should even consider using bottled water to brush your teeth. Make sure food has been thoroughly cooked and is served to you fresh and hot; avoid vegetables and fruits that you haven't washed (in bottled or purified water) or peeled yourself. If you have problems, mild cases of traveler's diarrhea may respond to Imodium (known generically as loperamide) or Pepto-Bismol. Be sure to drink plenty of fluids; if you can't keep fluids down, seek medical help immediately.

Infectious diseases can be airborne or passed via mosquitoes and ticks and through direct or indirect physical contact with animals or people. Some, including Norwalk-like viruses that affect your digestive tract, can be passed along through contaminated food. If you're traveling in an area where malaria is prevalent, use a repellent containing DEET and take malaria-prevention medication before, during, and after your trip as directed by your physician. Condoms can help prevent most sexually transmitted diseases, but they aren't absolutely reliable and their quality varies from country to country. Speak with your physician and/or check the CDC or World Health Organization Web sites for health alerts, particularly if you're pregnant, traveling with children, or have a chronic illness.

For information on travel insurance, shots and medications, and medical-assistance companies see Shots & Medications under Things to Consider in Before You Go, above.

DIVERS' ALERT
Do not fly within 24 hours of scuba diving.

SPECIFIC ISSUES IN LOS CABOS

In general, Los Cabos does not impose as great a health risk as other parts of Mexico. Nevertheless, watch what you eat and drink only bottled water or water that has been boiled for a few minutes. Water in most major hotels is safe for brushing your teeth, but to avoid any risk, use bottled water. Hotels with water-purification systems will post signs to that effect in the rooms.

When ordering cold drinks at establishments that don't seem to get many tourists, skip the ice: *sin hielo.* (You can usually identify ice made commercially from purified water by its uniform shape.)

Stay away from uncooked food and unpasteurized milk and milk products. *Tacos al pastor*—thin pork slices grilled on a spit and garnished with the usual cilantro, onions, and chili peppers—are delicious but dangerous. It's also a good idea to pass up *ceviche,* raw fish cured in lemon juice—a favorite appetizer, especially at seaside resorts. The Mexican Department of Health warns that marinating in lemon juice does not constitute the "cooking" that would make the shellfish safe to eat. Be wary of hamburgers sold from street stands, because you can never be certain what meat they are made with. That said, many travelers eat ceviche, street-stand tacos, and all the other wonderful foods that make dining in Mexico fun. If you're dining in a clean hotel or tourist-oriented restaurant, be a bit more adventuresome. Some travelers take a spoonful of Pepto-Bismol before eating as a precaution.

The major health risk, known as *turista*, or traveler's diarrhea, is caused by eating contaminated fruit or vegetables or drinking contaminated water. Mild cases may respond to Imodium (known generically as loperamide or Lomotil) or Pepto-Bismol, both of which can be purchased over the counter. Do not take Imodium or other antidiarrheal drugs for more than a day or two. If they don't cure the problem by then, you should definitely see a doctor. Drink plenty of purified water or tea; chamomile tea (*te de manzanilla*) is a good folk remedy and it's readily available in restaurants throughout Mexico. In severe cases, rehydrate yourself with Gatorade or a salt-sugar solution (½ teaspoon salt and 4 tablespoons sugar per quart of water).

▌ HOURS OF OPERATION

Banks are usually open weekdays 8:30–3. Government offices are usually open to the public weekdays 8–3; they're closed—along with banks and most private offices—on national holidays. Stores are generally open weekdays and Saturday from 9 or 10 to 7 or 8. In tourist areas, some shops don't close until 10 and are open Sunday. Some shops close for a two-hour lunch break, usually from 2 to 4. Shops extend their hours when cruise ships are in town.

HOLIDAYS

Mexico is the land of festivals; if you reserve lodging well in advance, they present a golden opportunity to have a thoroughly Mexican experience. Banks and government offices close during Holy Week (the week leading to Easter Sunday) and on Cinco de Mayo, Día de la Raza, and Independence Day. Government offices usually have reduced hours and staff from Christmas through New Year's Day. Some banks and offices close for religious holidays.

Official holidays include New Year's Day (Jan. 1); Constitution Day (Feb. 5); Benito Juárez's Birthday (Mar. 21); Good Friday (Friday before Easter Sunday); Easter Sunday; Labor Day (May 1); Cinco de Mayo (May 5); St. John the Baptist Day (June 24); Independence Day (Sept. 16); Día de la Raza (Day of the Race; Oct. 12); Dia de los Muertos (Day of the Dead; Nov. 2); Anniversary of the Mexican Revolution (Nov. 20); Christmas (Dec. 25).

Festivals include Carnaval (Feb.–Mar., before Lent); Semana Santa (Holy Week; week before Easter Sunday); Día de Nuestra Señora de Guadalupe (Day of Our Lady of Guadalupe; Dec. 12); and Las Posadas (pre-Christmas religious celebrations; Dec. 16–25).

▌MAIL

Airmail letters from Baja Sur can take up to two weeks to reach their destination. The *oficina de correos* (post office) in San José del Cabo is open 8–7 weekdays (with a possible closure for lunch) and 9–1 Saturday. Offices in Cabo San Lucas, La Paz, and Loreto are open 9–1 and 3–6 weekdays; La Paz and San Lucas offices are also open 9–noon on Saturday.

Post Offices **Cabo San Lucas Oficina de Correo** (⊠Av. Lázaro Cárdenas s/n ☎624/143–0048). **San José del Cabo Oficina de Correo** (⊠Mijares and Margarita Maya de Juárez ☎No phone).

SHIPPING PACKAGES

FedEx does not serve the Los Cabos area. DHL has express service for letters and packages from Los Cabos to the United States, Australia, Canada, New Zealand, and the United Kingdom; most deliveries take three to four days (overnight service is not available). To the United States, letters take three days and boxes and packages take four days. Cabo San Lucas, San José del Cabo, and La Paz have a DHL drop-off location. Mail Boxes Etc. can help with DHL and postal services.

Major Services **DHL Worldwide Express** (⊠Plaza los Portales, Hwy. 1, Km 31.5, Local 2, San José del Cabo ☎624/142–2148 ⊠Hwy. 1, Km 1, Centro Comercial Plaza Copan, Local 18 and 21, Cabo San Lucas ☎624/143–5202). **Mail Boxes Etc.** (⊠Plaza las Palmas, Hwy. 1, Km 31, San José del Cabo ☎624/142–4355 ⊠Blvd. Marina, Plaza Bonita Local 44-E, Cabo San Lucas ☎624/143–3032).

▌MONEY

Mexico has a reputation for being inexpensive, but Los Cabos is one of the most expensive places to visit. Prices rise from 10% to 18% annually and are comparable to those in Southern California.

Prices in this book are quoted most often in U.S. dollars, which are readily accepted in Los Cabos. Prices throughout this guide are given for adults. *For information on taxes, see Taxes.*

Prices throughout this guide are given for adults. Substantially reduced fees are almost always available for children, students, and senior citizens.

ATMS & BANKS

Your own bank will probably charge a fee for using ATMs abroad; the foreign bank you use may also charge a fee. Nevertheless, you'll usually get a better rate of exchange at an ATM than you will at a currency-exchange office or even when changing money in a bank. And extracting funds as you need them is a safer option than carrying around a large amount of cash.

■TIP➔**PIN numbers with more than four digits are not recognized at ATMs in many countries. If yours has five or more, remember to change it before you leave.**

ATMs (*cajas automáticas*) are commonplace in Los Cabos and La Paz; Loreto and Mulege also have an ATM. If you're going to a less developed area, though, go equipped with cash. Cirrus and Plus cards are the most commonly accepted. The ATMs at Banamex, one of the oldest nationwide banks, tend to be the most reliable. Bancomer is another bank with many ATM locations.

CREDIT CARDS

Throughout this guide, the following abbreviations are used: **AE**, American Express; **D**, Discover; **DC**, Diners Club; **MC**, MasterCard; and **V**, Visa.

It's a good idea to inform your credit-card company before you travel, especially if you're going abroad and don't travel internationally very often. Otherwise, the credit-card company might put a hold on your card owing to unusual activity—not a good thing halfway through your trip. Record all your credit-card numbers—as well as the phone numbers to call if your cards are lost or stolen—in a safe place, so you're prepared should something go wrong. Both MasterCard and Visa have general numbers you can call (collect if you're abroad) if your card is lost, but you're better off calling the number of your issuing

bank, since MasterCard and Visa usually just transfer you to your bank; your bank's number is usually printed on your card.

If you plan to use your credit card for cash advances, you'll need to apply for a PIN at least two weeks before your trip. Although it's usually cheaper (and safer) to use a credit card abroad for large purchases (so you can cancel payments or be reimbursed if there's a problem), note that some credit-card companies *and* the banks that issue them add substantial percentages to all foreign transactions, whether they're in a foreign currency or not. Check on these fees before leaving home, so there won't be any surprises when you get the bill.

■TIP➔**Before you charge something, ask the merchant whether he or she plans to do a dynamic currency conversion (DCC). In such a transaction the credit-card *processor* (shop, restaurant, or hotel, not Visa or MasterCard) converts the currency and charges you in dollars. In most cases you'll pay the merchant a 3% fee for this service in addition to any credit-card company and issuing-bank foreign-transaction surcharges.**

Reporting Lost Cards American Express (☎800/528–4800 in U.S., 336/393–1111 collect from abroad ⊕www.americanexpress.com). **Diners Club** (☎800/234–6377 in U.S., 303/799–1504 collect from abroad ⊕www.dinersclub.com). **Discover** (☎800/347–2683 in U.S., 801/902–3100 collect from abroad ⊕www.

discovercard.com). **MasterCard** (☎800/627–8372 in U.S., 636/722–7111 collect from abroad ⊕www.mastercard.com). **Visa** (☎800/847–2911 in U.S., 410/581–9994 collect from abroad ⊕www.visa.com).

REST ROOMS

Expect to find clean flushing toilets, toilet tissue, soap, and running water in Los Cabos. Other places should have simple but clean toilets. An exception may be small roadside stands or restaurants in rural areas. If there's a bucket and a large container of water sitting outside the facilities, fill the bucket and use it for the flush. Some public places, such as bus stations, charge one or two pesos for use of the facility, but toilet paper is included in the fee. Still, it's always a good idea to carry some tissue. Throw your toilet paper and any other materials into trash cans rather than the toilet in small businesses and remote areas that may have poor plumbing.

CURRENCY & EXCHANGE

The currency in Los Cabos is the Mexican peso (MXP), though prices are often given in U.S. dollars. At this writing, US$1 was equivalent to approximately MXP 10.5.

■TIP→ **Even if a currency-exchange booth has a sign promising no commission, rest assured that there's some kind of huge, hidden fee. (Oh…that's right. The sign didn't say no** *fee.***) And as for rates, you're almost always better off getting foreign currency at an ATM or exchanging money at a bank.**

WORST-CASE SCENARIO

All your money and credit cards have just been stolen. In these days of real-time transactions, this isn't a predicament that should destroy your vacation. First, report the theft of the credit cards. Then get any traveler's checks you were carrying replaced. This can usually be done almost immediately, provided that you kept a record of the serial numbers separate from the checks themselves. If you bank at a large international bank like Citibank or HSBC, go to the closest branch; if you know your account number, chances are you can get a new ATM card and withdraw money right away. **Western Union** (☎800/325–6000 ⊕www.westernunion.com) sends money almost anywhere. Have someone back home order a transfer online, over the phone, or at one of the company's offices, which is the cheapest option. The U.S. State Department's **Overseas Citizens Services** (⊕www.travel.state.gov/travel ☎202/501–4444) can wire money to any U.S. consulate or embassy abroad for a fee of $30. Just have someone back home wire money or send a money order or cashier's check to the state department, which will then disburse the funds as soon as the next working day after it receives them.

TRAVELER'S CHECKS & CARDS

Some consider this the currency of the caveman, and it's true that fewer establishments accept

EFFECTIVE COMPLAINING

Things don't always go right when you're traveling, and when you encounter a problem or service that isn't up to snuff, you should complain. But there are good and bad ways to do so.

Take a deep breath. This is always a good strategy, especially when you're aggravated about something. Just inhale, and exhale, and remember that you're on vacation. We know it's hard for Type A people to leave it all behind, but for your own peace of mind, it's worth a try.

Complain in person when it's serious. In a hotel, serious problems are usually better dealt with in person, at the front desk; if it's something quick, you can phone.

Complain early rather than late. Whenever you don't get what you paid for (the type of hotel room you booked or the airline seat you prereserved) or when it's something timely (the people next door are making too much noise), try to resolve the problem sooner rather than later. It's always going to be harder to deal with a problem or get something taken off your bill after the fact.

Be willing to escalate, but don't be hasty. Try to deal with the person at the front desk of your hotel or with your waiter in a restaurant before asking to speak to a supervisor or manager. Not only is this polite, but when the person directly serving you can fix the problem, you'll more likely get what you want quicker.

Say what you want, and be reasonable. When things fall apart, be clear about what kind of compensation you expect. That said, the compensation you request must be in line with the problem. You're unlikely to get a free meal because your steak was undercooked or a free hotel stay if your bathroom was dirty.

Choose your battles. You're more likely to get what you want if you limit your complaints to one or two specific things that really matter rather than a litany of wrongs.

Nice counts. This doesn't mean you shouldn't be clear that you are displeased. Passive isn't good, either. When it comes right down to it, though, you'll attract more flies with sugar than with vinegar.

Do it in writing. If you discover a billing error or some other problem after the fact, write a concise letter to the appropriate customer-service representative. Keep it to one page, and as with any complaint, state clearly and reasonably what you want them to do about the problem. Don't give a detailed trip report or list a litany of problems.

traveler's checks these days. Nevertheless, they're a cheap and secure way to carry extra money, particularly on trips to urban areas. Both Citibank (under the Visa brand) and American Express issue traveler's checks in the United States, but Amex is better known and more widely accepted; you can also avoid hefty surcharges by cashing Amex checks at Amex offices. Whatever you do, keep track of all the serial numbers in case the checks are lost or stolen.

Traveler's checks can be difficult to exchange in Mexico and are, therefore, not recommended.

American Express now offers a stored-value card called a Travelers Cheque Card, which you can use wherever American Express credit cards are accepted, including ATMs. The card can carry a minimum of $300 and a maximum of $2,700, and it's a very safe way to carry your funds. Although you can get replacement funds in 24 hours if your card is lost or stolen, it doesn't really strike us as a very good deal. In addition to a high initial cost ($14.95 to set up the card, plus $5 each time you "reload"), you still have to pay a 2% fee for each purchase in a foreign currency (similar to that of any credit card). Further, each time you use the card in an ATM you pay a transaction fee of $2.50 on top of the 2% transaction fee for the conversion—add it all up and it can be considerably more than you would pay when simply using your own ATM card.

Regular traveler's checks are just as secure and cost less.

Contacts American Express (☎888/412–6945 in U.S., 801/945–9450 collect outside of the U.S. to add value or speak to customer service ⊕www.americanexpress.com).

▌ SAFETY

Although the Los Cabos area is one of the safest in Mexico, it's still important to be aware of your surroundings and to follow normal safety precautions. Everyone has heard some horror story about highway assaults, pickpocketing, bribes, or foreigners languishing in Mexican jails. Reports of these crimes apply in large part to Mexico City and other large cities; in Los Cabos, pickpocketing is usually the biggest concern.

■TIP→ **Distribute your cash, credit cards, IDs, and other valuables between a deep front pocket, an inside jacket or vest pocket, and a hidden money pouch. Don't reach for the money pouch once you're in public.**

▌ TAXES

Mexico charges an airport departure tax of about US$10 or the peso equivalent for international and domestic flights. This tax is usually included in the price of your ticket, but check to be certain. Traveler's checks and credit cards are not accepted at the airport as payment for this fee.

A 2% tax on accommodations is charged in Los Cabos, with proceeds used for tourism promotion.

Baja California Sur has a value-added tax of 10%, called I.V.A. (*impuesto de valor agregado*), which is occasionally (and illegally) waived for cash purchases. Other taxes and charges apply for phone calls made from your hotel room.

▌ TIME

Baja California Sur is on Mountain Standard Time.

▌ TIPPING

When tipping in Los Cabos, remember that the minimum wage is the equivalent of $3 a day and that the vast majority of workers in the tourist industry live barely above the poverty line. However, there are Mexicans who think in dollars and know, for example, that in the United States porters are tipped about $2 a bag; many of them expect the peso equivalent from foreigners but are sometimes happy to accept 5 pesos (about 5¢) a bag from Mexicans. They will complain either verbally or with a facial expression if they feel they deserve more—you and your conscience must decide. Following are some guidelines. Naturally, larger tips are always welcome.

For porters and bellboys at airports and at moderate and inexpensive hotels, $1 per bag should be sufficient. At expensive hotels, porters expect at least $2 per bag. Leave $1 per night for maids at all hotels. The norm for waiters is 10% to 15% of the bill, depending on service (make sure a 10%–15% service charge hasn't already been added to the bill, although this practice is more common in resorts). Tipping taxi drivers is necessary only if the driver helps with your bags; 50¢ to $1 should be enough, depending on the extent of the help. Tip tour guides and drivers at least $1 per half day or 10% of the tour fee, minimum. Gas-station attendants receive 30¢ to 50¢, more if they check the oil, tires, etc. Parking attendants—including those at restaurants with valet parking—should be tipped 50¢ to $1.

INDEX

NOTES

NOTES

NOTES

NOTES

NOTES

NOTES

NOTES

NOTES

NOTES

NOTES